PRAISE F
CREATI
AND THE CRAFT OF TEACHING

"In *Fire in the Classroom: Creativity, Entrepreneurship, and the Craft of Teaching*, Ray Smilor's consummate skill has produced a book that frees teachers to be more creative, inspires in them the courage to light fires in their courses, laboratories, and projects, and equips them with the tools to unleash the creativity of their students."

—**Norval C. Kneten**, senior advisor, Council of Independent Colleges; former president, Barton College, Wilson, North Carolina

"*Fire in the Classroom* is a great book. I love the way Smilor weaves major thinkers and creators into the examples of creative, successful teaching. I appreciate the way he uses classic movies, references to well-known books and authors like Shakespeare, John Gardner, Peter Drucker, Stephen Covey, and Walter Isaacson, and analogies to river rafting, jazz, improvisation, and the butterfly effect, to enhance topics that will inspire teachers!"

—**Tahita Fulkerson**, founding president, Trinity River Campus, Tarrant County College, Fort Worth, Texas

"*Fire in the Classroom* will spark the curiosity of any teacher, whether a teaching assistant, a newly minted PhD, or a tenured professor. Ray Smilor writes as he teaches—with enthusiasm for the job and respect for the student. I recommend this book to anyone considering teaching as a profession, or to anyone deep in the throes of academic teaching already. Follow the guidelines that Smilor provides through his infinite wisdom and candor, and you are bound to help students discover a heated passion for learning."

—**Dr. Suzanne Carter**, professor of practice in strategy and executive director, EMBA program, Texas Christian University; president, board of directors, Texas Women in Higher Education (TWHE)

"Dr. Ray Smilor is a master teacher who exemplifies the fire in the classroom. His insights and guidance in *Fire in the Classroom: Creativity, Entrepreneurship, and the Craft of Teaching* offer a roadmap for all educators to follow to craft their skills."

—**Dr. Donald F. Kuratko**, Jack M. Gill Distinguished Professor of Entrepreneurship, the Kelly School of Business, Indiana University–Bloomington

"*Fire in the Classroom* is a wonderful journey on which I feel privileged to have gone; every educator should give themselves the gift of reading it. As a teacher, I came away more grounded than ever in the importance of my craft. As a colleague, I came away touched by Smilor's thinking and inspired to grow. And, because he reminds us that teaching is a human endeavor, I came away deeply hopeful about the future. Teaching has always had me jumping out of bed at 5 a.m. without need for an alarm clock. But this book has given meaning to my passion and provided a powerful lens for me to think about what I do as a craft with the potential to change the world."

—**Dr. Alex Bruton**, former teaching professor, engineering and entrepreneurship, University of Calgary; cofounder and chief transformation officer, Educators Pro

"Great teaching is about impacting lives. And every great teacher has their own distinct style for doing so. In *Fire in the Classroom: Creativity, Entrepreneurship, and the Craft of Teaching*, Smilor shares the secrets that are commonly practiced among teachers who not only touch the minds but also the hearts and souls of their students."

—**Dr. Michael Morris**, professor, entrepreneurship and social innovation, Keough School of Global Affairs, University of Notre Dame

"Ray Smilor has done the teaching profession a great service with this book. He has identified the four requirements of great teachers: a deep knowledge of their chosen field; a commitment to their students as customers and learners; an ability to deliver content in ways that enable each student to learn; and a passion to continually improve as a teacher.

Fire in the Classroom includes stories, exercises, and suggestions that will be useful to any teacher. I wish he had written this book years ago."

—**Dr. Jana Matthews**, ANZ chair in business growth; director, Australian Centre for Business Growth, University of South Australia

"*Fire in the Classroom* is a treasure trove of diverse teaching and learning gems that combines inspiration, philosophy, and pragmatism. Ray Smilor not only inspires readers to be better teachers, but he also provides valuable perspectives and insights on the craft of teaching while always offering practical tools, techniques, and next steps for teachers. Great stuff!"

—**Greg Fisher**, Larry and Barbara Sharpf Professorship in Entrepreneurship, Department of Management and Entrepreneurship, Kelley School of Business, Indiana University–Bloomington

"I absolutely loved *Fire in the Classroom*; Ray Smilor is such a wonderful storyteller. I wish I had read this early in my career. But even for someone who is as seasoned as me, I was still inspired. Countless faculty and their students will benefit greatly from Smilor's willingness to share his journey and wisdom."

—**Dr. Rebecca White**, James W. Walter Distinguished Chair in Entrepreneurship; director, John P. Lowth Entrepreneurship Center, Sykes College of Business, University of Tampa

"*Fire in the Classroom: Creativity, Entrepreneurship, and the Craft of Teaching* is a beautifully crafted book that shows a path that leads to authentic learning experiences. Smilor reinstates the noble profession of teaching and provides a successful guide for any teacher to excel in the classroom."

—**Dr. Sunil Shukla**, director, Entrepreneurship Development Institute of India

Fire in the Classroom

Fire in the Classroom

Creativity, Entrepreneurship, and the Craft of Teaching

Ray Smilor

ROWMAN & LITTLEFIELD
Lanham • Boulder • New York • London

Published by Rowman & Littlefield
An imprint of The Rowman & Littlefield Publishing Group, Inc.
4501 Forbes Boulevard, Suite 200, Lanham, Maryland 20706
www.rowman.com

86-90 Paul Street, London EC2A 4NE, United Kingdom

British Library Cataloguing in Publication Information Available

Library of Congress Cataloging-in-Publication Data

Names: Smilor, Raymond W., author.
Title: Fire in the classroom : creativity, entrepreneurship, and the craft of teaching / Ray Smilor.
Description: Lanham, Maryland : Rowman & Littlefield, [2022] | Summary: "Fire in the Classroom focuses on innovative ways teachers can enhance the creativity of their courses to make the learning process for themselves and their students more engaging and productive. It shows teachers how to help students take advantage of opportunities and create value in their discipline by thinking and acting more entrepreneurially"—Provided by publisher.
Identifiers: LCCN 2022018310 (print) | LCCN 2022018311 (ebook) | ISBN 9781475867657 (cloth) | ISBN 9781475867664 (paperback) | ISBN 9781475867671 (epub)
Subjects: LCSH: Teacher effectiveness. | Entrepreneurship—Study and teaching. | Motivation in education.
Classification: LCC LB1025.3 .S6135 2022 (print) | LCC LB1025.3 (ebook) | DDC 371.102—dc23/eng/20220713
LC record available at https://lccn.loc.gov/2022018310
LC ebook record available at https://lccn.loc.gov/2022018311

To my sons, Matthew Wesley and Kevin Raymond, who taught me how to be a father, and to my granddaughters, Natalie Elaine and Samantha Erin, who are teaching me how to be a grandfather. And, of course, always to Judy Ann, my entrepreneurial partner in life.

"For the mind does not require filling like a bottle but rather, like wood, it only requires kindling to create in it an impulse to think independently and an ardent desire for the truth." —Plutarch

Contents

Foreword

My first teaching job was similar to Ray Smilor's. I taught third grade at Oaklawn Elementary, a school in the same district where I had attended elementary school myself. Teaching third grade for three years was one of the most exciting experiences in my life. While I learned a lot about my students, I also learned a lot about myself. Specifically, I reflected on the values that drove my decisions regarding my students and their needs. I also learned about the critical roles that family and community play in students' learning and lives. And finally, I learned about the impact that instruction, curriculum, and assessment can have on students and their futures.

Unlike me, though, Ray continued to grow in his teaching expertise, shifting from elementary school to middle school and then to the university level. At first, he taught undergraduates and, later, graduate students in the field of business. During these years, Ray began exploring the area of entrepreneurship.

At the time, entrepreneurship as a formalized field of instruction did not exist, and thus there were neither seminal textbooks nor college degrees available to students and teachers who were interested in the topic. In short, there was very little to connect entrepreneurship with teaching and learning. Aware of this gap, Ray Smilor began experimenting with innovations in both entrepreneurship and teaching. His considerable efforts led him to formulate a set of guiding principles that have grounded his understanding of teaching and learning.

Three principles, in particular, stand out. First, preparation is essential for anyone hoping to achieve excellence in teaching. With preparation, teachers can understand a subject and confidently teach it to others while anticipating the challenges that students will have upon first encountering it. Second, Smilor encourages teachers to listen. For example, by engaging with mentors, both novice and expert teachers can expand their knowledge base. The third principle is that a passion for teaching can greatly strengthen students' engagement in their learning content.

Anyone who reads Dr. Smilor's book *Fire in the Classroom: Creativity, Entrepreneurship, and the Craft of Teaching* will undoubtedly develop a much deeper understanding of what it means to be a teacher. The book will help K–12 teachers understand the importance of preparation and will, in turn, ignite a passion for learning in their youngest students.

Teachers at the undergraduate level will learn how their passion for subject matter can profoundly shape the career choices and lifelong learning of young adult students. And teachers who work with adult learners of any age will gain greater insights into the value of being innovative in their teaching.

Those who read this book will also encounter the compelling argument that the beliefs and experiences of teachers are not superior to those of students. In fact, Dr. Smilor reminds us that students are not empty vessels waiting to be filled. Instead, students come to class with diverse beliefs and experiences that are critical to their own learning and, indeed, to the learning of their peers and teachers. Thus, teachers need to find ways to leverage this mix of beliefs and experiences so that all the participants in a classroom feel engaged with both the teaching and the learning.

Additionally, Dr. Smilor's book challenges us to think deeply about our students and to reflect on complex questions: Who do my students think I am? And who do I think my students are? These types of questions, by allowing for deep reflection, raise higher levels of awareness for teachers who care about their craft. This book's primary purpose is to ignite a love for learning and to promote deep thinking and innovation in relation to the classroom. The book is divided into four sections, with each section grounded in the impressive and varied experiences of the author.

The first section, "Teaching and Learning," reminds the reader about the connections between these two fundamental elements of education.

Dr. Smilor emphasizes the extent to which teachers can learn from mentors, including other teachers.

The second section, "Creativity and Teaching," challenges teachers to be innovative and to remember that we all possess an innovative side. This section also highlights how creativity is contagious in ways that strengthen students' willingness to explore new worlds.

The book's third section, "Teaching for Excitement," provides teachers with explicit practices that endow teaching and learning processes with meaning and even excitement. The section encourages us to consider the decisive role that experiential learning can play in the interactions between teachers and students.

The final section, "Beyond the Classroom," focuses on—and offers fascinating examples of—how teachers, over years and even decades, can maintain their passion for the craft of teaching and their commitment to their students.

Anyone who reads *Fire in the Classroom* is in for a treat. Dr. Smilor takes complex issues related to teaching and learning, explores them in relation to his own experiences, and presents an inspiring resource with which teachers can creatively and enthusiastically improve every aspect of classroom life.

Frank Hernandez
Dean and Professor of Educational Leadership
College of Education, Texas Christian University
founding member, Deans for Impact

Preface

A Mighty Purpose

This book is about finding and following a mighty purpose.

The great Irish playwright George Bernard Shaw profoundly observed: "This is the true joy in life, the being used for a purpose recognized by yourself as a mighty one." His point serves as a revelation for teachers. It doesn't make any difference what others might think about your mighty purpose in teaching in a discipline that you love. It should only make a difference to you. So whether you come to think of your mighty purpose as a worthwhile, motivating, energizing, and meaningful one, it should make no difference to others, as long as it makes a difference to you.

The book ahead explains how I came to find my mighty purpose in teaching, how that purpose has affected what I do and how I do it, and why it has made a difference for me. The chapters that follow focus on the process of becoming a teacher, describe practices to enliven the classroom, and identify ways to make teaching a more meaningful and creative experience for both teachers and their students.

My hope, as you read this book, is that your own mighty purpose in teaching becomes a bit clearer, that you gain insights into the craft of teaching, and that you come to appreciate more fully the joy of teaching.

Through a circuitous route, I became a teacher, which surprises me. More astonishing to me is that I am a teacher of entrepreneurship. Most people think that entrepreneurship is about starting a business. Certainly, one outcome of entrepreneurship could be starting and building a successful business.

Entrepreneurship, however, is much more than that. It is about living a more fulfilling life, utilizing one's creative and innovative talents, and finding purpose and passion in what one does. It is essentially about pursuing opportunity in whatever career or discipline one chooses to work.

One can think and act entrepreneurially in a large corporation as an "intrapreneur," or become a social entrepreneur in a not-for-profit organization, or act entrepreneurially in a government post or in one's place of worship and one's community. As this book shows, a teacher can even be an academic entrepreneur. Entrepreneurial teachers can upset the status quo, alter accepted ways of doing things, and transform classrooms. In the process, they can find meaning for themselves and for those whom they teach.

If there is a philosophy for the field of entrepreneurship, it is "Carpe diem." Seize the day! The chapters ahead show how teachers can seize the teaching day by enhancing their skills in the craft of teaching.

THE CRAFT OF TEACHING

Like other crafts, teaching requires dexterity, ingenuity, and even artistry.

More than ever today, teachers need to hone their skills in curriculum design and implementation, improve the effectiveness of their performance in the classroom, and take pride and satisfaction in the creativity of their courses. The chapters here help teachers learn to become better at their craft.

By focusing on their craft, teachers have the opportunity to address the learning styles of every one of their students and to spark the imagination of others by doing something that they love. They have at their disposal a range of tools and techniques that they can work to master to create meaningful and memorable learning experiences. This book is designed to share with current and aspiring teachers' perspectives to assist them in becoming more confident, accomplished, and inspired in implementing their craft.

Harvey Penick, the great golf coach, taught some of the most successful stars on the Professional Golf Association Tour and the Ladies Professional Golf Association Tour. On one occasion, he was attending a championship event when one of his pupils stopped to talk with him before her tee time. As her tee time approached, she got up and said to Mr. Penick: "I have to go play now." He lightly touched her arm to keep her a moment longer so he could remind her, "You don't *have* to go play. You *get* to go play. There's a world of difference."

Teachers who become better at their craft never say that they have to go teach. They constantly remind themselves that they *get* to go teach. They *get* to share their experience; they *get* to provide insight and inspiration; they *get* to promote the lessons and competencies of a discipline that they love; they *get* to influence their students in a positive way; they *get* to teach! What a difference when considering the craft of teaching!

Introduction

A Teacher's Journey and the Book Ahead

My journey as a teacher began as a job, developed into a career, and emerged into a calling. At every educational level at which I have taught, I have learned lessons about the craft of teaching. These lessons are woven into the organization of this book and reflected in the practice of teaching in the chapters ahead.

AT THE ELEMENTARY LEVEL

My first teaching job was on the elementary level at the Texas School for the Deaf in Austin, Texas, in 1969. I had never taught before and did not have the foggiest notion of what a teacher was supposed to do. There is an adage that advises to "fake it till you make it." But I didn't even know enough about teaching to figure out what I needed to fake.

The school hired me because I was fluent in sign language after serving as a houseparent manager in one of the cottages for a year. In addition, I had demonstrated that I could communicate effectively with teenage boys, and the school was looking for more role models, especially for teenage boys. So, the school's administrators took a chance on me. Surprises me even today that they did.

Fortunately for me, another teacher became a mentor to me just when I needed one the most. She provided a crash course to me in teaching and got me as ready as she could. I had a few things going for me that gave hope that I would not be a disaster and that I might even be able to be an actual teacher.

I listened and learned. I asked questions, even the dumb ones, and applied what she recommended. I took her advice on how to set up the room, on writing and revising the lesson plan for the week, on preparing materials and activities to utilize during the class day, on ways to assess performance, on how to keep a grade book, on how to anticipate disciplinary situations, on how to keep students engaged. During that first week and first month, she came by to observe me every day, and we had an evaluation session at the end of each day.

Just as important, I had a lot of energy. I enjoyed being in the classroom and relished the challenge of keeping the attention and engagement of each and every student. I liked the performance element of teaching.

IN JUNIOR HIGH SCHOOL

After earning my Texas teacher's certificate, I then taught English and social studies to seventh and eighth graders in the Austin Independent School District for two years while working on my PhD at the University of Texas at Austin (UT).

These kids were rambunctious, spontaneous, and willing to try new things. And they taught me. I learned the importance of the "teachable moment"—that unexpected opportunity for reflection and insight that was off script from the lesson plan. I began to look for more teachable moments in every teaching setting thereafter.

AMONG UNDERGRADUATES

After I completed all my course work for my PhD in US history at the University of Texas at Austin and became ABD (all but dissertation), I taught American history for a few semesters—my first foray into college teaching. I began to experiment with alternate teaching techniques like using slide shows (this was before PowerPoint) to set a tone for a situation (like Matthew Brady's powerful photographs of Civil War battles) or music to reinforce a historical period, like the jazz era of the

1920s. I did not realize it at the time, but I was beginning to address the different learning styles of the students in the class—the importance of which I would come to realize much later.

My most unexpected undergraduate teaching opportunity came six months after I became a research assistant in the new IC^2 Institute (which stands for Innovation, Creativity, and Capital) at the Graduate School of Business at the University of Texas at Austin in 1979.

The chair of the management department asked me to teach the required Principals of Management course to undergraduates. So, I bought the textbook and volunteered to teach the 7:30 a.m. course to a class of 220 students. I taught that course for three years and achieved a key goal—no one slept through a single class. Energy and enthusiasm for what one is teaching (and learning), I discovered, can enhance the classroom experience (or at least keep students awake).

I then designed and taught the first high-technology marketing class at the school. The class required creating content for the new field of emerging technologies, such as information systems, biotechnology, and nanotechnology.

IN EXECUTIVE EDUCATION

During this same time, I began to teach in the Executive Education Programs at UT. These were two-to-four-hour sessions on specific topics like customer-driven marketing, designing great customer service, and enhancing creativity in organizations for groups of experienced executives as part of their continuing management and leadership development.

The executives in the program were (and are) a demanding audience. I benefited from every chance to interact with them because they required that I be prepared, flexible, and responsive to their learning requirements and expectations.

Two key components to teaching emerged through these teaching experiences. One is substance; the other is form. The first requires creating content—assembling information and insights in new and sometimes unconventional ways, bringing theory and practice together, identifying and sharing what people and organizations were doing and why they were doing it.

The second emphasizes the performance element—being "onstage," facilitating lively discussions, engaging others actively in the learning process, trying out different learning techniques, and having fun doing it.

GRADUATE EDUCATION AND A CALLING

Then in 1985, I was asked to start an entrepreneurship curriculum for the MBA program in the Graduate School of Business at UT. At the IC^2 Institute, I had been doing research on entrepreneurial companies, writing books about how entrepreneurs start and grow companies, and organizing national and international conferences on fast-growth enterprises.

No entrepreneurship discipline existed at the time. There were no textbooks on entrepreneurship, no doctoral programs granting degrees in entrepreneurship, few materials to present in class, and little theory and practice related to teaching entrepreneurship. In other words, it was a perfect area for someone with a degree in history to begin to develop a program in an emerging academic discipline! The field was wide open for experimentation and innovation for someone from the outside, whose only real credentials were a fascination with this new field and a willingness to jump into it.

These teaching and researching experiences shaped my evolution as a teacher and led me to find my mighty purpose in the teaching of entrepreneurship. They also resulted in three key lessons about the craft of teaching that have influenced the design of this book:

There is no substitute for preparation. Having a firm grip on the material, thoroughly knowing what one is planning to do, anticipating what may happen, and reviewing content over and over again all make for a more productive teaching and learning experience.

Listen to others with more knowledge and experience than yourself. Their insights, know-how, and lessons learned improve one's own performance. Humility in assessing one's capabilities goes a long way toward improving them.

Energy forgives a lot of sins. Energy and enthusiasm are force multipliers in the classroom and can be contagious.

THE BOOK AHEAD

While I am a teacher of entrepreneurship, this book is designed for anyone who teaches any subject. The content is organized around a clear and overriding purpose. In this case, it is to show that education should not be about "filling a bottle." It should be about "kindling" a fire for learning.[1] Teachers in any discipline should try to inspire and not just inform, work to challenge and not just dictate, encourage independent thinking and not just memorization, and ignite creative and innovate ways to unleash an ardent desire to learn in every student. When they do, they can spark fires in their classrooms.

This book revolves around four sections, each contributing to the overriding purpose.

The first section involves "Teaching and Learning." Like the chicken-and-egg causality dilemma, which comes first in the classroom, the desire to learn or the willingness to be taught? Both seem necessary for both the student and the teacher. The three chapters in this section show how teaching and learning go hand in hand; one contributes to and depends on the other. No one is a born teacher. By gaining experience, learning from other teachers, with the help of mentors and by seizing on the teachable moment, a teacher learns how to manage a class, orchestrate a curriculum, apply effective teaching techniques, influence the lives of their students in a positive way, develop their own teaching style, and eventually recognize and pursue their own mighty purpose.

The second section deals with "Creativity and Teaching." Are only a few of us really creative? Are all the rest of us simply incapable of tapping into the apparent magic of the creative process? Or, is every student creative and capable of magical acts of imagination? The chapters in this section demonstrate how teachers engender a classroom for creativity, spark a recognition that their course is different and intriguing, and show their students how to deal positively and innovatively with the unexpected.

The third section discusses "Teaching for Excitement." The three chapters in this section focus on specific techniques that teachers can use to make the learning process more meaningful, more interesting, more compelling, and more fun for their students. It shows how the supposedly "boring" lecture can be personal, exhilarating, and creative for both the teacher and the student. It explains how to use the been-there, done-that experience of outside speakers to enliven the classroom. It points out how powerful experiential learning can be.

The fourth section looks "Beyond the Classroom." How do teachers sustain their passion, enthusiasm, and commitment to their craft and their students over time? What can teachers do to continue to be excited about their own mighty purpose? This section highlights how motivating the role of mentor can be to a teacher and points out ways for teachers to seek inspiration, sustain curiosity, and provide hope for their students.

Each section ends with "Takeaways." These are thoughts for further consideration, reflections to think about after reading the chapters in this book. What are the possible actions that you might like to apply to your teaching situation and to your own mighty purpose as a teacher?

The appendix provides detailed instructions for teachers to implement the activities and exercises that the book describes.

The result can be a classroom on fire.

A classroom on fire releases "an impulse to think independently and an ardent desire for the truth," to quote the Greek philosopher Plutarch. It employs active teaching strategies that utilize the power and excitement of experiential learning. It recognizes the potential and unleashes the creativity of each student.

A classroom on fire makes learning personal, meaningful, and enjoyable by emphasizing self-reflection and self-awareness. It sparks a student's curiosity through investigation and discovery, encourages critical thinking by challenging assumptions, and promotes risk taking and the pursuit of opportunity through experimentation.

In a classroom on fire, teachers communicate their own passion for and commitment to their disciplines. They apply their own creative talents to design innovative courses that inspire and motivate their students. They take renewed joy in honing their craft of teaching.

SECTION I

Learning and Teaching

Chapter 1

Becoming a Teacher

Like the chicken-and-egg causality dilemma, there is the learning-and-teaching causality dilemma. Which comes first? Does one's desire to learn spark the willingness to be taught? Or does teaching light the fire for learning? Clearly, both seem necessary.

This dilemma is at the heart of whether one decides to pursue a job, a career, or a possible calling in teaching.

THE FORK IN THE ROAD

One of Robert Frost's most famous poems is "The Road Not Taken." The traveler in the poem comes upon two roads that lie ahead of him, and he must decide which path to take at the fork. He opts for one, thinking he might come back for the other one sometime in the future. But he doesn't. The path that the traveler chooses eventually leads to meaning and purpose. But what exactly helps him to choose?

The unconventional American philosopher of the twentieth century Yogi Berra put this choice another way. In one of his most noted Yogiisms, he advised, "When you come to a fork in the road, take it!"

For a teacher, how does one take the fork that leads to a meaningful and purposeful teaching path?

Three factors influence the decision:

- *Consider the push and the pull.* The push is driven by necessity. Perhaps one needs a job, and a teaching position becomes available. Or, one is dissatisfied with their current work environment or dislikes their boss or becomes bored with their immediate routine and increasingly feels pushed into something else, perhaps teaching. Or, a person is just unhappy with and unfulfilled by their station in life and begins to seek something that could be more meaningful, and teaching appears an attractive alternative.

The pull is driven by opportunity. A position in teaching appears to be an irresistible chance to do something exciting, to launch a creative career direction and to make a difference in one's life and in the lives of others. The pull implies future possibilities both personally and professionally. Considering both the push and the pull can influence one's decision to opt to teach and can sometimes work in tandem as one decides which fork in the road to take.

- *Identify one's gift.* What is it that we do that we really enjoy and that we are really good at? Once a person identifies their gift, then can teaching let them do more of that? The interesting issue about one's gift is that a person usually downplays it. The assumption is that if one is good at something and really enjoys it, then everyone must be. Assuming that this is the case is a mistake.

  Perhaps one's gift is deep empathy for others or outstanding organizational skill or the ability to marshal information and communicate it effectively or a talent to present to others or a knack for solving problems or excitement for a specific topic. One can determine their gift by their own self-reflection, by taking a series of self-assessment tools and by talking with others who know them well. The key is to not underestimate one's gift and then to see how that gift might be applied to teaching.

- *Pose a key question.* In considering a path of teaching, ask, "How will I feel if I don't do this?" If, after considering the influence of the push and the pull and after identifying one's gift, a person is comfortable not pursuing a teaching position, then well and good. However, if after thinking of those factors, one poses the question and then decides that they would always regret not trying, then the path to teaching becomes clearer.

A PERTINENT ARGUMENT

Once choosing the path of teaching, then a teacher confronts the causality dilemma of teaching and learning. To appreciate the implications of this dilemma to teachers, it is useful to consider it first in the context in the discipline of business. There is an old argument in the field of entrepreneurship that is pertinent to teaching. Can entrepreneurship be taught? Successful entrepreneurs answer almost always, not just "No." But "Hell, no!" Entrepreneurs, they would claim, were "born." Usually, academics in other established disciplines would argue the same thing. "Just can't teach entrepreneurship," they would maintain. So, are successful entrepreneurs "born" or are they "made"?

The hidden assumption in this argument is that there is only a small, select number of people who have what it takes to think and act entrepreneurially and to actually start and build enterprises. Most people, the argument went, simply could not learn the basics of venture development and did not have the secret sauce (whatever that might be) to succeed at their own enterprises or even perform entrepreneurially in any kind of organization. Only a lucky few, the can't-teach-entrepreneurship lobby insisted, had the inborn passion, chutzpah, and ability to actually think and act entrepreneurially and to create a successful venture.

Yet evidence abounds that lots of people, younger and older, men and women, from all kinds of backgrounds and upbringings, do indeed launch and build their own enterprises. Additional evidence shows that people in all kinds of organizations—for-profit and not-for-profit, large corporations and start-ups, governmental and nongovernmental entities, and even academic environments—perform as intrapreneurs in solving problems, generating creative and innovative ideas, and launching internal enterprises. How is that possible?

Once, it was argued that management skills couldn't be taught. A good manager was a "born manager." But today of course, teaching management is something we take for granted. At one time, a similar debate raged about leadership. Yet today, we have courses and programs to make people better leaders.

Entrepreneurs are not born. The human genome has been mapped, and there is no chromosome in one's DNA stamped with an "E" for entrepreneur. So something else must be at work in the development of entrepreneurs. It is a combination of learning and teaching.

Just as in the push-and-pull assessment, entrepreneurs can be either "opportunity driven" or "necessity driven." In the former, the entrepreneur recognizes an opportunity based on a potential customer's need or problem and then is driven to find out how to address that need or problem effectively. In the latter, the entrepreneur, perhaps from losing one's job or facing changed personal conditions, finds it necessary to do something to change the situation in which they find themselves.

In both cases, teaching and learning come into play. Every entrepreneur demonstrates "fire in the belly." That is the wellspring of drive and passion that gives meaning to one's entrepreneurial efforts and that spark the need and desire to *become* an entrepreneur.

Rather than ask the question "Can entrepreneurship be taught?" perhaps a better question is "Can entrepreneurs learn?" When asked the learning question, successful entrepreneurs give the same response: "Yes, and let me tell you what I want to learn, what I need to learn, and what I wish I had learned earlier and faster."

What we know about the entrepreneurial process is this: successful entrepreneurs are exceptional learners who are willing to be taught, if that teaching—from other entrepreneurs, from scholars, from experience, and from teachers of entrepreneurship—helps them in their own entrepreneurial endeavors.

The teaching and the learning focus on a range of competencies to think and act entrepreneurially, including the abilities to identify, assess, and pursue opportunity; to demonstrate creativity and innovation in addressing challenges, needs, and problems; to marshal limited resources; to communicate a compelling vision; to build effective networks; and ultimately to create value for themselves and for those with whom they come in contact.

Entrepreneurship education thus focuses on experiential learning. Because entrepreneurship is about doing something that creates value, the performance-based curriculum of entrepreneurship focuses on what one does as well as on what one knows. Thus, one becomes an entrepreneur by learning (and being taught) how to do an opportunity assessment, how to pitch an idea, how to prepare a lean start-up, how to write and present a business plan, how to do an entrepreneurial audit of an organization, and how to bootstrap a new venture, among other experienced-based learning initiatives.

People *become* entrepreneurs. Entrepreneurship can be taught, and entrepreneurs can learn.

BECOMING A TEACHER

The born-versus-made argument about entrepreneurship applies to teaching in general. Really great teachers are "born" to teach, so the argument goes. Somehow, there is a select group of teachers who are naturally gifted in the classroom, and the rest are just hangers-on who can't find anything better to do.

There is an old and mean adage that argues, "Those who can, do; and those who can't, teach." This adage is usually offered up by those enamored of their own success and disdainful of anyone else who helped them get where they are. They credit their own ability to learn while disparaging whatever others have taught them. When they actually encounter a good teacher, then they maintain that the teacher is an exception to the rule and "born" to teach.

Great teachers are not born. Individuals may exhibit empathy for others, may display energy and enthusiasm for a topic, and may demonstrate skill in communicating with others. But the craft of teaching requires more than that.

One must also become expert in one's discipline; be able to combine theory and practice; actually construct a meaningful course with classes that build on one another; know how to address the different learning styles of each student; understand how to deal with the learning disabilities of some of their students; maintain the attention, interest, and enthusiasm of their students throughout the learning process; and ultimately create value for their students and themselves.

In other words, one becomes a teacher. The becoming occurs through study and practice, through formal and informal means, by interacting with and being taught by other teachers, by developing one's own teaching style, through self-reflection, via constructive critique by others, and by assessing what works and what does not.

Recognizing what one is becoming can be an enlightening discovery. Norman Maclean notes the importance of this awareness in his book

A River Runs through It: "One of life's quiet excitements is to stand somewhat apart from yourself and watch yourself becoming the author of something beautiful."[1]

Only by combining their own learning with a willingness to be taught do teachers become adept at the craft of teaching.

Chapter 2

Learning Styles

Becoming a teacher who lights fires and doesn't just fill buckets requires an important recognition. People learn differently. That is, they have different learning preferences. Therein lies the difference between a teacher who just informs and one who inspires.

The Golden Rule advises to treat others as one would like to be treated. That is well and good as far as it goes. However, it is not quite as effective or meaningful as a corollary to that advice, which recommends to treat others as they would like to be treated. In other words, instead of focusing on one's own preferences in how to be treated, it is much more powerful and impactful to focus on the preferences of others.

For a teacher, the issue is significant. One approach would be to maintain that a teacher should teach others as the teacher would like to be taught. But the result of that approach would be to miss a real learning opportunity for any student in a teacher's class who does not prefer to learn the way the teacher does.

Rather, a better, more engaging, and more impactful approach to the classroom is for a teacher to teach others as they would like to be taught. That is, a teacher should structure their lectures, activities, exercises, and assignments in such a way that they address the preferred learning style of each and every student in each and every class.

How can a teacher do that? To start, a teacher must admit that their students don't necessarily like or prefer to learn the way the teacher does. Ignoring the way other people learn can leave students bored, confused, and lost. Paying attention to the learning styles of others can spark the desire to learn, make the classroom more fun, and leave students wanting more.

The Kolb Experiential Learning Profile (KELP) is a critical teaching tool in becoming a more gifted and more fulfilled teacher. KELP is a self-assessment tool that identifies four major learning styles or preferences: diverging, assimilating, converging, and accommodating. The profile also provides insights on how to address these different learning styles in the classroom so that each student becomes more engaged in the learning process and so that teaching becomes more interesting, stimulating, and useful.[1]

DIVERGING STYLE

Students with a diverging style learn by combining feeling with watching. They like to learn through personal involvement with people. They are sensitive to the feelings of others and work to understand how others feel about things. They rely more on feelings than on developing systematic approaches to problems and situations. They are open minded. They enjoy involving themselves in new experiences. They prefer to observe rather than take action. Thus, they excel at recognizing problems, gathering data, generating alternatives, and brainstorming.

For divergent learners, a teacher can present opportunities to run simulations and other gaming programs, conduct consulting projects, provide research opportunities, participate in internships, make presentations, interview role models, discuss alternates to situations in case studies, listen to guest lecturers, and get involved in team projects.

ASSIMILATING STYLE

Students with an assimilating style learn by combining watching and thinking. They like to analyze data and work to understand the implications coming from a wide range of information. They have a talent for contemplating and defining problems and are adept at putting information into concise, logical form that is easier to understand and digest. They are good at planning and are more focused on abstract ideas and concepts than on people. Thus, they are strong at forming theories and models, and they like to learn from models.

To address this learning style, a teacher can present the theory behind the practice and use models to convey important concepts. In addition to responding to innovative teaching methods such as movie clips and YouTube videos, these learners like to listen to lectures, enjoy analyzing problem situations, are open to special reading assignments and thought papers, and are good at developing plans for team projects.

CONVERGING STYLE

Students with a converging style learn by combining thinking and doing. They find practical uses for ideas and like testing models and theories. They are problem solvers. They prefer to deal with problems and technical tasks rather than social or personal issues. They use logic and reasoning in addressing situations and are comfortable setting and working toward goals. They use a hands-on approach to make decisions.

A teacher can implement a range of learning techniques to capture the attention and interest of converging learners. These learners respond to interactive lectures, exercises that require experimentation and testing of concepts, reviews of theoretical concepts, case study discussions that have technical issues to address, hands-on projects, and team assignments that require practical applications.

ACCOMMODATING STYLE

Students with an accommodating style learn by combining doing and feeling. They like hands-on experiences. They take initiative to get things done and enjoy carrying out plans. They favor new challenges in which they can act on their intuition rather than logical analysis. They rely more on people for information than on logical analysis. They can envision possibilities in various situations, are comfortable using trial and error to come up with practical solutions, and enjoy working in groups.

To address this learning style, a teacher can focus on active experimentations in the classroom, exercises that require hands-on experiences, group projects and tasks, interactions with experts in a particular field, assignments that require personal initiative, evaluations of organizations, and discussions of decision-making in case studies.

THE AGILE LEARNER

The goal over the course of a semester is to have the students—and the teacher—become more agile learners. While everyone has a preferred learning style in which they are most comfortable learning, agile learners develop the ability to learn through every style, not just the one that is dominant for them.

As KELP points out, the agile learner progresses through a cycle of experiencing, reflecting, thinking, and acting. Teachers can help their students become more agile learners by having them do or have an experience in their classroom, review or reflect on that experience, conclude or learn from the experience, and then plan or try out what they have learned.

The teacher who lights fires consciously structures their classes to address each learning style while also helping students improve their abilities to learn in any style. By having students with different styles work together, by showing students how to value other people's learning styles, and by helping students strengthen the learning areas in which they are weaker, a teacher can not only enhance the learning experience in their own classrooms but also better prepare students for lifelong learning.

Chapter 3

The Teachable Moment

Teachable moments lie hidden in the unexpected. Waiting in the recesses of the surprising, lingering in the openings of the unconventional, and gathering outside the limitations of the predictable, there are amazing learning experiences to be found. The issue for any teacher looking for the teachable moment is whether they actually recognize what the unexpected provides.

The teachable moment is never in a syllabus, can't be found in a lesson plan, and never appears in a PowerPoint. It lurks unannounced and unanticipated behind structured classes, detailed outlines, and thorough planning. One cannot locate it in a scripted lecture, a neatly organized presentation, or a well-directed case study.

Rather, the teachable moment appears suddenly and unexpectedly. It comes out of nowhere to surprise both teacher and students. It disrupts the best of plans, redirects the most carefully crafted lessons, and alters the direction of a class. By its stunning unexpectedness, it can make the routine exceptional, transform the commonplace into the extraordinary, and make learning profound.

But only if a teacher recognizes the moment and then takes advantage of it.

Time and again, the teachable moment appears as an anomaly. There is something out of place that captures a teacher's attention, something different that sparks wonder, and something unusual that captures one's curiosity. Therein often lies the difference between excitement and boredom in the classroom, between a course that captures the imagination of students and one that dulls it, and between a teacher who inspires and one who simply informs. The issue is whether a teacher seizes on the anomaly.

An old adage advises to "expect the unexpected." Most of the time, however, teachers don't. Most of the time they ignore the unexpected or shun it because it violates their assumptions, or goes against their preconceived notions, or interrupts their lesson plan, or gets in the way of what they think they are supposed to teach or are mandated to teach. Teachers forge ahead to cover the material. Shouldn't they get through all the slides in their PowerPoint? Isn't it necessary to cover everything in the textbook? Why stop to discuss the unexpected when they have to review everything that will be on the test?

Richard Feynman, the Nobel laureate in physics, provides a key insight about the teachable moment and the power of the unexpected. He profoundly observes, "The thing that doesn't fit is the thing that's most interesting, the part that doesn't go according to what you expected."[1]

Feynman seizes on the anomaly. He wants us to pay attention to the surprising and unanticipated. He advises that we focus not on what we expect to find but on what we don't expect to find. He argues that it is in the unexpected that real learning takes place, that it is in the unanticipated where we learn something valuable that we were not aware of previously. In that moment, we learn something valuable about ourselves, experience something enlightening about a topic, reassess how we think about something, and know the joy of discovery.

Evidence of the impact on learning by recognizing and acting on the unexpected abounds. In science, the arts, and business, paying attention to the anomaly can lead to amazing results.

Spence Silver, a chemist at 3M, was charged with developing a glue for a stronger adhesive. But he accidentally created a weaker adhesive. Instead of ignoring the unexpected, he became fascinated with the glue that would not stick. The result was the Post-It Note, one of 3M's most wildly successful products.[2]

In a study of the bacterium staphylococcus, Alexander Fleming noticed that a penicillium mold spore had accidentally found its way to a petri dish that in turn inhibited bacterial growth. Instead of ignoring the accident, he became enamored of how it had happened. In the process of his investigation, he discovered the world's first broadly effective antibiotic substance, which he called penicillin and which has saved millions of lives.[3]

A remarkable example of recognizing and acting on the unexpected is related to the Tiger Woods juggling-golf-ball commercial. Nike hired Doug Liman, a Hollywood director of such actions films as *The Bourne Identity* and *Edge of Tomorrow*, to shoot a commercial featuring Woods to launch Nike's new line of golf equipment. The idea for the commercial was to have three golf duffers waiting to tee off when Woods asks to join them. The duffers suddenly become amazing golfers hitting incredible shots just by being in Woods's presence. When Woods has to leave the group, the duffers return to being terrible high handicappers.

During a break in the shooting, Liman noticed Woods just playing with a golf ball by tapping it with a sand iron behind his back, under his legs, and then hitting it like a batter hits a baseball. He was astounded by Woods's almost magical ability with a golf club. Instead of ignoring this moment, he took a camera, walked over to Woods, lay down on the ground, and asked Woods to duplicate his sorcery for twenty-eight seconds, the length of a commercial. Woods accomplished it on the fourth take. Liman added music and the Nike swoosh at the end. In the process, he created one of the most iconic commercials on television.[4]

How easy would it have been for Liman to ignore Woods and just get back to shooting the original commercial? Hadn't Liman had a contract with Nike to complete the planned assignment? Why take the time and effort to go off script?

Silver, Fleming, and Liman became captivated with the anomaly. The unanticipated somehow sparked their curiosity. They all paid attention to something they did not expect to discover, and therein lay an amazing opportunity to discover and to learn.

In the classroom, teachable moments lead to learning. Is a teacher willing to stop and ask, "What if?" What if they pursue that question? What if they discuss that topic? What if they try that experiment? Maybe something interesting and important happens.

Teachers who light fires are always on the lookout for the teachable moment. They accept spontaneity. They don't know when or how it might emerge, but they realize how powerful a learning experience it can be. They seek to make the most of the unexpected when it occurs. They want to be ready to set aside the planned agenda, turn off their PowerPoint, or shift the focus of a discussion to take advantage of the surprising question, the unanticipated conflict, and the inquisitive experiment.

The teachable moment occurs at every level of education. Each time, it makes the learning process engaging, exciting, and memorable for both the students and the teacher.

An eighth-grade teacher of English recognized and took advantage of the teachable moment. In a lesson on playwriting, teams of four students had to create and then perform a five-minute play in the classroom. One team asked the teacher if they could use "cuss" words such as "damn" and "hell" in their dialogue. The teacher discussed with them the importance of being judicious in their word selection and then permitted them to go ahead with their play.

The team began their performance with a loud banging on the classroom door as one of the actors shouted, "Damn it! Who the *hell* is knocking on the damn door?" For the next five minutes, the team apparently set the world record (perhaps still unbroken) for the number of times the words "damn" and "hell" appeared in a short play. A concerned teacher from across the hall came rushing over and asked if everything was okay. "Yes," the teacher replied, "aspiring playwrights at work."

Instead of simply going on to the next play, the teacher focused the class on what had just occurred. The result was a discussion with the entire class about the importance of words, about the use of language to enhance or inhibit the impact of what one says, about how people react to what they hear, and about what makes for a really good or bad play.

In the discipline of entrepreneurship, teachable moments occur in a variety of ways: actually talking directly with customers about their needs and wants, testing and sometimes failing in the development of a new product or service, having one's business plan critiqued by experienced investors, debating a key decision point in a case study, challenging an assumption about organizational behavior. When teacher and students seize on the teachable moment, plan A becomes plan B; a product or service takes on new meaning; an idea becomes a genuine opportunity.

To recognize the teachable moment in the unexpected and to discover something one does not set out to discover, a teacher should do the following:

- *Pay attention to the anomaly.* Identify what is unexpected and surprising, and then focus on it. What is behind the difference of opinion? Pick up on the contrary point of view. Emphasize the "aha" insight in a case study observation.

- *Avoid preconceived notions.* Approach students, the classroom, and the learning environment with an open mind. Don't ignore the anomaly or try to excuse it away. Seize on the surprising and make it part of the learning experience. Stop to explore a conflict among students, different points of view on a current event, or an unconventional approach to an assignment.
- *Consciously look and listen.* A teacher should ask, "What am I really seeing? What am I really hearing?" Seek the "why" behind the "what." Why did a student ask that question? What is behind a student's unusual comment or observation?
- *Be ready to pivot.* Expect to set aside the lesson plan, the organized lecture, and the well-planned agenda in order to follow up on the spontaneous. Look for the clash with the usual. What is unique in a presentation or a team project? What student behavior reinforces a key principle or violates a key value? Therein lies an opportunity for discussion and learning.
- *Be curious.* Get excited about what is really different and unusual. Be willing to try something a student suggests, even when it is outside the planned agenda or assigned task. Highlight for the class an intriguing insight, a telling story, or an insightful revelation from a student's project or written report.
- *Extend the learning.* Responding to the unexpected is not a one-off event. Utilizing the teachable moment creates new teaching opportunities in the classroom. A creative teacher works the learning experience of the unexpected into the next class they teach on the topic, thus expanding the range of examples available to them to reinforce what they are teaching.

The teachable moment follows where the unexpected intrudes. If a teacher pays attention to the anomaly, avoids preconceived notions, consciously looks and listens, and shows curiosity, their teachable moment becomes an electric and rejuvenating experience not only for their students but also for themselves.

Section I

Learning and Teaching

Takeaways

Section I has focused on "Learning and Teaching." It has emphasized that teachers are not born but made. They become expert at their craft over time through study and practice, through formal and informal means, by interacting with other teachers, and by their own desire learn in combination with their willingness to be taught.

Part of that learning process for teachers is to become more aware of the different learning styles of their students and then implementing strategies, techniques, and assignments that address those learning styles to help their students become more agile learners.

One essential component to fully engage students and to make the classroom experience more exciting and impactful is for a teacher to recognize and act upon the teachable moment—those unexpected, off-script opportunities for discovery and learning.

Think about three takeaways related to how teaching and learning have interacted for you. What struck you as interesting, surprising, and/or applicable to your situation? Consider: How have you learned your area of expertise? What has influenced you in your search for a calling? What teachable moments have you had?

Specific takeaways might include: assessing the push/pull factors that influenced your choice of a calling in teaching and evaluating how pertinent they are now; identifying your unique gift(s) and considering how you can use it/them more directly in your classes; focusing on a teachable moment from your class and considering what you would do differently when the next teachable moment occurs.

SECTION II

Creativity and Teaching

Chapter 4

The Creative Classroom

Are there only a few among us who are actually creative? Only a minuscule number of us who can think and act creatively? Is creativity somehow doled out sparingly and haphazardly to random lucky ones? Does it apply to just a handful of painters, sculptors, and musicians? Or can creativity emerge in all of us in all kinds of conditions, careers, and callings?

There is something magical about the creative process. Bursts of imagination can seem to appear as if out of thin air. Solutions to complex problems can seem to jump out like pulling rabbits from a hat. Is this process the domain of only a few David Copperfields? Or are each and every one of us capable of apparently dazzling acts of magic?

Teachers who spark the creativity of their students begin each course and every class with a key assumption: all of their students—each and every one of them—are wonderfully, marvelously, incredibly gifted people who have the innate drive, curiosity, and ability to design, develop, and deliver acts of remarkable creativity. If only all teachers believed that!

There is a disabling myth about creativity. The myth is, *most people are not creative . . . including ourselves*! When asked, "Who is creative?" most people assume they are not. They are captives of a myth. The job of a teacher in whatever discipline they teach is to convince their students otherwise.

ORIGINS OF THE MYTH

In a kindergarten classroom on parent-teacher night, a large flip chart hung from the ceiling in one of the rooms. It emphasized the three rules of coloring. Under each rule were three graphics to demonstrate the rule, and under each of those graphics was a critique to indicate pleasure or displeasure about following the rule:

- *Rule 1, "Stay in the lines."* Three heart-shaped images appeared below the rule. The first showed the color red scratched all outside the lines of the heart with a sad face below it. The second indicated some coloring outside the lines of the heart with a neutral face below it. The third heart was colored perfectly within the lines with a happy face below it.
- *Rule 2, "Make the white go away."* Three balloons appeared below the rule. The first balloon showed a lot of white space and a sad face below it. The second balloon showed some white space with a neutral face below it. The third showed a balloon perfectly colored in blue with no white space and a happy face below it.
- *Rule 3, "Use colors that make sense."* Below the rule were three trees. The first tree was colored purple with a sad face below it. The second tree was colored yellow with a neutral face. The third tree was of course green with a happy face underneath it.

Before reading these directives, a person would not be aware that there were such strict rules about coloring and such judgments about not following them. Without these rules, students would not recognize that coloring outside the lines was such an offense and would not appreciate that leaving any white space was a prohibition. They would not realize that some colors made sense and that others were somehow senseless. The message from this class seemed to be that there would be no Picassos or Van Goghs or Pollocks in this classroom.

One source of the widespread belief that we are not creative is our educational system, which from our earliest experience often tells us that there is only one right way to do something, that there are certain rules that must be followed at all times, that we must stay within strict guidelines to be right. No wonder that so many begin to think that they are incapable of being creative.

These boundaries that the educational system puts around people are often reinforced in the work environments in which they find themselves. While most organizations give lip service to looking for new ideas and creative alternatives, they are actually quite resistant to them. People at all levels in organizations come up with good ideas all the time. They like generating solutions to problems and finding innovative approaches to improving organizational performance.

But often, and with the best of intentions, leaders and managers get very good at killing those ideas and in the process diminishing not only idea generation but especially the enthusiasm of others to even try to suggest something new.

When someone proposes a new idea, they often encounter classic put-downs under the guise of helpful suggestions: "We don't have the budget for that"; "We tried something like that once before, and it didn't work"; "The boss will never go for it"; "That's not our business"; "We don't have the time and the people to consider that"; "We have never done that around here." Or they will be turned away by clichés disguised as insights: "Don't rock the boat"; "That will never fly"; "If it ain't broke, don't fix it." No wonder people with ideas start to doubt their creative abilities.

Worse than that, they begin to doubt themselves and worry about what others will say about them. Instead of taking a chance on offering a new idea, they become fearful. Given the put-downs they encounter, they wonder if they will be embarrassed in front of others. Will they look silly or foolish or ridiculous or stupid? Best to put their ideas aside and say nothing.

How should teachers counter restrictive educational systems and negative workplace environments when it comes to creativity? How do they create classrooms that actually help each and every student recognize and utilize their own creative talents?

WILLING TO BE WRONG

Sir Ken Robinson, the outstanding scholar and author on education and creativity, provides direction on these questions. In his insightful TED talk on "Do schools kill creativity?" he defines creativity simply and powerfully as ideas that have value.[1] It is the teacher's responsibility to support and encourage those ideas. Since ideas are opportunities in the making, the only way to find out where the opportunities might lead is to pursue them.

In pursuing ideas, Robinson provides an essential insight about creativity that is key to a creative classroom. He argues that to be creative one must be "willing to be wrong." Unless one is willing to be wrong, nothing creative can occur. Unless one is willing to be wrong, fear of looking ridiculous or ignorant prevents a person from trying something new or suggesting an alternative course of action or offering a different opinion on an issue.

Robinson tells the delightful story of a little girl in art class. The teacher gives the students an assignment to draw a picture of someone famous. While all the students start immediately to draw, one little girl appears to be thinking carefully before she begins to draw. Intrigued, the teacher goes to the girl and asks, "What famous person are you drawing a picture of?" The girl replies that she is drawing a picture of God. "But," the teacher says, "no one knows what God looks like." The girl replies, "They will in a minute!" By being willing to be wrong, she will come up with something creative.

How do teachers encourage this kind of courageous attitude? One key way is to devise teaching exercises, techniques, and approaches that require students to be willing to be wrong.

For example, often on the first day of a class, a teacher might conduct an exercise called "half of thirteen" by simply asking students, "What is half of thirteen?" (What would your answer be?)

Whether the students are high school students, or undergraduates, or executives, the first answer is always six and a half. After congratulating them on this response, the teacher asks, "What else is half of thirteen?" After a brief surprise that there might be another answer, someone will say 6.5. Praising the answer, the teacher asks again, "What else is half of thirteen?" The class will often propose other mathematical solutions such as thirteen divided by two.

Eventually, someone will dare to offer the proverbial thought from left field, such as one and three (thus dividing the number thirteen between the one and the three). Recognizing that this is an awesome answer, other students will divide the number 13 horizontally and diagonally. Soon the floodgates open. Others begin to offer unconventional suggestions such as "thir" and "teen" (which opens potential answers to dividing other languages), or 06:30, which invokes military time, or half a baker's dozen, which ties in donuts. Then someone may propose something really interesting by connecting the answer to roman numerals, which elicits answers such as eleven, two, and eight.

This exercise demonstrates a critical point about creativity and teaching. After a teacher steers away from the accepted, obvious, taught, and "correct" answer, students become more willing to be wrong and, in the process, begin to be more creative. Students are often taught in school that there is one right answer, but in reality, there is never just one answer. There is always more than one way to solve a problem or take advantage of an opportunity or devise something new, if one is willing to be wrong.

The role of the teacher in this exercise is important. What happens if, when a student proposes a response like "one" and "three" for half of thirteen, the teacher responds, "That is a stupid answer. Don't you know the correct answer? Everyone knows the right answer is six and a half!" Suddenly, all discussion stops. Immediately, no one ventures to be wrong. The creative thinking ends. Instead, the teacher takes a more creative role as nonjudgmental in the idea generation process, as encouraging of new thinking, as rewarding of unconventional thoughts, as constantly pushing for additional alternatives. (See exhibit 1 in the appendix.)

CONCEPTUAL BLENDING

We tend to think that great ideas come from something that no one has ever thought about before. That somehow to be creative, one must have a burst of imagination springing from something that no person has ever considered in the past. Not so. Instead, leaps of creativity often come by blending concepts together, by linking up two thoughts that others have considered but putting them together in a new and unconventional way. Arthur Koestler, the historian and economist, actually coined a term for this conceptual blending phenomenon. In his book *The Act of Creation,* he calls it "bisociation."[2]

Bisociation is the ability to connect the unconnectable, to relate the unrelatable, to put two wildly different things together in an unexpected way. The result is the "aha" sensation of a new and unanticipated idea.

Bisociation is powerful, Koestler contends, because it surprises and intrigues us. It also is a source of delightful humor.

Koestler tells the story of a Texas rancher traveling through the state of Missouri. The rancher stops at a Missouri farm to talk to a farmer who is sitting in his rocking chair on his front porch. Pretty soon, the discussion gets around to talking about the size of the farm. The rancher asks the farmer, "How big is your farm?" The farmer pulls on his chin and pointing replies, "Well, if you go from the edge of my porch, to that big oak tree, then go over to that rock wall, then cross the road, then walk up to that far fence post, then cross over the creek on the right and then come back to my porch, that's my farm."

The rancher smirks a bit and tells the farmer, "Well, on my ranch in Texas, I can get in my car at dawn, travel all day long, and at nightfall I'm still not at the other end of my property." The farmer thinks for a minute and then says, "You know, I used to own a car like that!" The farmer's bisociative connection is cars and property, and the ability to relate the two surprises and pleases us.

Bisociation happens all the time. Late night talk show hosts use it constantly in their monologues. They make us laugh because we don't expect the unanticipated relationships that they connect. Marketers often depend on bisociation for their television ads. Consider Super Bowl commercials such as when Betty White gets tackled in the mud before eating a Snickers bar, or the Budweiser Clydesdales play football, or a beaver saves a motorist from a flood by emphasizing tires. Bisociation applies to company names like Apple for a computer company or 1–800-Flowers for a florist shop. It applies to technology breakthroughs as when George de Mestral made a connection between how cockleburs stick on socks and the development of Velcro.

In other words, creativity happens when we make unusual connections. Teachers can help their students learn how to do that.

"Round objects" is an exercise that demonstrates how our brains actually can make unusual connections almost automatically for us. The exercise starts with a simple and fun directive, "Make a list of round objects." Students then have ninety seconds to make their list. Invariably, everyone starts with balls: baseball balls, golf balls, bowling balls, soccer balls, table tennis balls, and so on until they exhaust their list of balls. They always list balls first because our image of roundness and balls is most obvious and, as it turns out, least creative.

After exhausting their list of balls, students start to tap their bisociative abilities. Their list moves to other round objects like coins, planets, and fruit. Then their bisociative inclinations become more wide ranging as they consider wildly different kinds of round objects like eyes, manhole covers, rings, wheels, bullets, pizza, and so on. Eventually, some will come up with round objects that are not quite round at all but quite original, such as the movement of comets, tornadoes, and puckered lips, thus connecting the unconnectable.

What begins as something quite common and ordinary becomes amazingly unconventional and diverse. After discussing the variations and the implications of their lists, students count the number of items they listed. There are always a few who display an impressive count of twenty or more items in just ninety seconds, which allows the teacher to discuss the concepts of drive and persistence in pushing through on a creative idea. (See exhibit 2 in the appendix.)

LEARN FROM MISTAKES

One other element is necessary for the creative classroom. Teachers need to help students recognize that failure is not an end but just another kind of learning experience.

Thomas Edison experimented constantly in seeking to find solutions to problems. When asked about the many failures he had encountered during his wide-ranging investigations, he replied, "I have not failed ten thousand times. I've found ten thousand ways that didn't work." This attitude toward failure is intriguing and essential in helping students appreciate their creative talents. How we label something influences how we feel about the experience and in turn affects how we act. One of Edison's guidelines for his work was "Fail your way to success." Edison has 1,093 patents, still the individual record.[3] For Edison, failure was just another kind of learning experience.

People actually experience failure all the time, although they don't tend to call it that. Instead, they may refer to it as trial and error. When something doesn't work the first time, they make a revision, improvise or try another approach, and then try again and again until they find a solution. That's creative.

An exercise called "dots" easily demonstrates how comfortable students can be with trial and error, which is simply failing and then trying again. In dots, students are asked to draw a straight line, without lifting their pencil from the paper, which will cross through nine dots arranged in a tic-tac-toe pattern. They try again and again until someone discovers the solution. Then they are asked to do it with three lines, and then, in a surprise, to do it with one line through all nine dots.

Eventually, a wide range of solutions emerge after trial and error, as students may cut up the paper and line up the dots, roll up the paper and utilize a circular line, or use a much wider marker instead of a narrow pencil. Throughout this exercise, students don't view their attempts as failures but rather as learning experiences of what doesn't work. (See exhibit 3 in the appendix.)

The movie *Apollo 13* recounts the harrowing journey of the three-member crew of astronauts who encountered problems in their command module that prevented them from landing on the moon and endangered their lives on the way back to Earth. In one memorable scene called "Square Peg in a Round Hole," the NASA engineers in Houston discover that the lunar module, in which the astronauts are now riding, is running out of oxygen and the level of CO_2 is increasing. If they are not able to reverse this process, the crew will die of carbon dioxide poisoning. It is a problem that the engineers had never imagined happening.

In the critical scene, the lead NASA engineer gathers his team in a room, dumps a box of items on the table, and explains that this is all they have to work with inside the capsule. He then tells his team that they must find a way to make a rectangular "scrubber" canister, which was designed to filter out carbon dioxide in the command module, to fit the circular canisters in the lunar module (and thus the square-peg-in-a-round-hole analogy). Through trial and error, they come up with a contraption that actually works and saves the lives of the three astronauts.[4]

ACTIVE INVOLVEMENT AND ENGAGEMENT

The creative classroom can be chaotic, ambiguous, and uncertain. But if students are actively involved and engaged, it is never boring. Teachers should want their students to have the chutzpah, confidence, and tools to be willing to be wrong by experimenting, asking questions, sharing their own experiences, and disagreeing—even with them. Teachers can engender a creative classroom by following a few key guidelines when students come up to them and say, "I have an idea":

- *First, try not to say no.* If a teacher wants their students to be willing to be wrong, then they must be as well. Consequently, the teacher must take on the role as guiding them to further investigate their idea. They can make suggestions about how to get additional information, set up contacts with others who may be able to assist them, and allow them to test their idea as part of their class learning.
- *Second, provide access to other resources.* A teacher can help students make connections to people with different backgrounds and knowledge, introduce them to organizations that might be useful in their assessment of their idea, and recommend ways to enhance their research efforts.
- *Third, focus on learning.* No matter what students may conclude about the viability of their idea, a teacher can help focus them on understanding what they have learned along the way by facilitating their own self-reflection through discussion, feedback from fellow students, and written "experience memos," in which they detail their own learning.

By their willingness to be wrong, by their ability to make bisociative connections, and by learning from trial and error, students may in fact begin to realize and apply their own magical creative talents.

Chapter 5

Anything Different Is Good

At the end of the movie *Groundhog Day*, Phil Connors the weatherman, played by Bill Murray, wakes up to the sound of "I Got You Babe" playing on the radio as he has done for seemingly countless mornings as he has repeated the same day over and over again. Then, the radio disc jockey interrupts the song. Phil looks perplexed. What is happening? He then feels the arm of Rita Hansen, the television producer, played by Andie MacDowell, across his chest. Phil pinches her arm to find out if it is real or imagined. The pinch wakes Rita up. Phil says, "Something is different." Rita asks, "Good or bad?" Phil responds, "Anything different is good."

This is the mantra of creative teachers. *Anything different is good.*

Being really different in the classroom generates enthusiasm in students, engages them in an active learning experience, and builds an environment for creativity and innovation. In many classes, students fall into a routine that they come to expect to be the norm in all classes that they take. They listen to the instructor, take notes, complete assignments, take tests, and then move on to the next class.

In these classes not much learning takes place, and there is certainly not much enthusiasm for the topic. Students and their teacher soldier through the semester in a kind of forced march. The teacher faithfully follows the textbook and then administers midterm and final exams that are often multiple-choice tests. If a student is really good at memorizing data, then they can ace both tests for easy As and then immediately proceed to forget most of what they had memorized.

On the other hand, teachers who teach courses that actually come to mean something to students and that stay with them after the course is over inspire by their interactivity, their outside-the-classroom assignments, their willingness to let students focus on something that is personally important to them, and the personal interest that the teacher takes in them. There is something remarkably different with these teachers and these types of courses.

Teachers in these creative courses violate the expectations of their students at every turn in the teaching process and in every way that they can. They want their students to think, "Oh, this is really different!" They want to surprise them with the unexpected, engage them with the unanticipated, and involve them with the unconventional.

THE INVITATION

Anything different is good starts before a class begins with an unconventional email invitation to the course. The teacher who wants to design a creative classroom communicates to their students that they are excited to have the opportunity to teach—and to be taught by—each one of them. Such an invitation sets the stage for and encourages students to bring their best thinking, highest energy, and most creative abilities to the class.

To get students to think outside the proverbial box, even before the first class, such an invitation alerts students to coming attractions in the course such as experiential exercises, interactive lectures, individual and team assignments, and competitions. It entices them with things to look forward to over the semester, even suggesting games and prizes for some class activities!

The precourse invitation might even add, "But wait, there's more!"

Through the invitation, students begin to realize that they will have the opportunity to reflect on learning that is important to them personally. They learn that they will be given tools and resources to think and act creatively.

Importantly, a precourse invitation like this also asks students to create their own to-learn list by identifying three or four learning objectives of their own. What is it that they want to learn in the course that is personally, powerfully, and emotionally important to them? A teacher who sends this type of email invitation to their class wants students to start thinking of their responsibility for their own learning.

To develop an invitation like this, a teacher should follow a know-feel-do approach to shaping the communication. The teacher should let students know some key elements of the course that they can expect to experience. The invitation should aim to make them feel excited, a little anxious and curious about what they are getting into. It should require them to take action by creating their own to-learn list. By putting all this together, a teacher should hope and expect that the reaction to their course, even before students step into it, is "Oh, this is really different."

Students rarely get an invitation to a class like this. With a genuine desire to share their own enthusiasm, a touch of humor, and a bit of tongue-in-cheek commentary, a teacher can surprise and intrigue students who are about to come into their course. They can cause students to wonder, given how unusual the invitation is, what must the actual course be like? Even more intriguing, what must the teacher be like? (See exhibit 4 in the appendix.)

THE SYLLABUS

An iconic police procedural drama from the 1950s, *Dragnet*, still plays on television. Each week, Sergeant Joe Friday, a Los Angeles police detective played by Jack Webb, investigated crimes and apprehended the criminals who committed them. The show became a cultural police drama phenomenon, setting the example for all police crime dramas to follow. In each episode, Sergeant Friday, while interviewing witnesses to the crimes, had a memorable phrase that he would deliver with a stone face and a deadpan voice: "Just the facts, ma'am. Just the facts." Or, "Just the facts, sir. Just the facts." In other words, skip any emotion; avoid digressions; don't elaborate.

Most course syllabi follow Joe Friday's directive. "Just the facts, students. Just the facts." Joe Friday would have been pleased with the syllabi that most faculty put together. These syllabi list the course title, indicate the office hours, offer a brief and formal description of the course, note the assignments, explain the grading system, and present the schedule. "Just the facts, students. Just the facts." A syllabus does not have to be like this.

A syllabus can and should want students to say of a course, "Well, this is really different!" For that to happen, a teacher must redefine what a syllabus is and what a syllabus is supposed to do. At its most basic level, a syllabus is an outline of the topics that a teacher will cover in a course. But that is woefully inadequate to communicate how dynamic, exciting, and creative a course can be.

Instead, a syllabus can tell a compelling story full of drama, excitement, action, and adventure. It can read more like a novel than a simple outline. From the start to the finish, the syllabus should surprise students with how different it is. For all that to happen, a teacher must reimagine what it says and how it says it.

To begin, a teacher should communicate their role and why they are passionate about the topic that they teach. A teacher's metaphor defines how they view themselves in the classroom. It reimagines their relationship with their students. Is a teacher simply an instructor, or is there a more meaningful way for a teacher to view themselves? In this regard, a teacher may see themselves as an orchestra conductor harmonizing the different talents of their students, or a gardener planting seeds to blossom and grow later, or a sage providing wisdom from experience.

Consider the metaphor of a "guide" for the journey that both teacher and students are about to begin. A guide provides direction for a journey that includes dealing with the unknown, covering new territory, and experiencing novel situations.

To reinforce a metaphor, a teacher can include favorite quotes in the syllabus to inspire and not just inform. A teacher may quote Apple's "Think Different" commercial from 1997, which touches on almost every discipline: "Here's to the crazy ones . . . they change things. . . . And while some may see them as crazy ones, we see genius. Because the people who are crazy enough to think they can change the world are the ones who do." (Then show that commercial on YouTube on the first day of class.)

A demonstration like this can help set up the journey of the course and actually tells students that this course could be really different.

As the syllabus (and the story) unfolds, it lets students know what the journey ahead may be like. Will it be experiential throughout, surprising and unexpected at times, quite ambiguous now and then, intense on occasion, challenging and demanding most of the time, personally revealing, and potentially highly rewarding?

To deal with these possibilities, a teacher may point out what students can expect to encounter: experiential exercises, interactive lectures, case studies, individual and team projects, readings, YouTube "live" videos, and guest speakers. What the teacher is actually informing students about is that the course will utilize a range of techniques, methods, and approaches to address the learning styles of everyone in the class.

The schedule in the syllabus is not just a listing of class times and topics, but instead a kind of educational GPS to navigate the learning journey. It sets out the direction that teachers and students will be headed, shows the passage of time, alerts students to potential forks in the road, and identifies key decision points that they will face. In such a narrative, assignments become the rivers they will ford and the mountains they will climb.

To help them traverse this landscape, the teacher can provide detailed rubrics that serve as essential clues for success for each of the assignments, which may include class contribution, reflective essays, a written team project, and a formal team presentation.

A syllabus can even include cartoons to increase awareness of important themes. For example, a cartoon of two spiders at the end of a playground slide can encourage students to dream big and persist. The spiders have stretched their flimsy web across the bottom of the slide. One spider says to the other, "If we pull this off, we'll eat like kings!"

A syllabus is also a contract. The teacher is committing to do what they say they will do—to show up for each and every class fully prepared, enthusiastic, and responsive; to provide thoughtful and quick feedback; to grade fairly; and to treat each student with dignity and respect. Students for their part make a similar commitment—to show up for each and every class fully prepared and enthusiastic, to complete assignments, and to bring a positive attitude to each session.

As part of the contract, the syllabus includes key policies of the university that both the teacher and the students must follow to ensure the academic integrity of the school. Any academic misconduct, such as cheating, plagiarism and collusion, will not be tolerated. After students read and reflect upon this type of syllabus, a teacher hopes they will say, "Oh, this course is different."

THE FIRST DAY

To put the mantra *Anything different is good* to the test so that students actually believe the course is different, the first day of class is important.

Most classes start with a conventional routine. The teacher writes their name on the board; describes their credentials by mentioning their experience, awards, degrees, and/or publications; and then proceeds to use the rest of the first day of class to review the syllabus with an emphasis on the assignments and the grading. First day done! Can't there be a better and more creative start?

Consider an alternative beginning for a teacher. Start with music playing. Perhaps One Republic's "Good Life" for its beat, words, and implication for the course. The song is about finding a way to live a good life, which is what students aspire to. Then, personally greet each student (or as many as possible in a larger class) and welcome them to class.

Even more impactful is to memorize all (or most) of the names of the students in one's class by studying their pictures after downloading the class list. Students are surprised, to say the least, that a teacher may already know them by name before the class begins. The combination of the music and knowing the students by name sets the expectation for the unexpected. A good start.

Before a teacher says anything about themselves, they could conduct a brief experiential exercise, such as half of thirteen or list of round objects. The purpose is to get students engaged immediately, interacting with one another, tossing out ideas, and reflecting on what they are experiencing.

Instead of introducing themselves through the typical information about experience and credentials, a teacher could do a "bag resume." This activity involves pulling six or seven objects from a brown grocery store bag that describe the key influences in the teacher's life. After that unconventional perspective, a teacher could give each student a bag to introduce themselves that way in the next class.

As the first class winds down, a teacher can touch on the syllabus (assuming that the students have already read it), review the journey ahead, answer questions, consider the to-learn lists of the students, and focus on the expectations that the students have for the course.

A different and compelling start to a course from the norm.

DURING THE COURSE

When a teacher commits to *Anything different is good*, something interesting occurs as the course continues. Students don't just come to expect the unexpected. They look forward to it. "What will happen today?" they wonder. They bring an increasing willingness to participate in discussions, to show a positive attitude in experiential exercises, and to ask questions (even the supposedly dumb ones). In other words, they get more comfortable taking a risk, venturing an opinion, moving outside their comfort zones, and demonstrating their creativity.

Music plays an important role in this process. But not just any music. For music to be most effective, it should reflect the topic or theme of a particular day's class. For example, if a case study focuses on whether a person should start their own company or remain with their firm, the song playing when students enter the classroom could be "Should I Stay or Should I Go" by the Clash. Students get the connection right away as they enter.

The theme from *Mission Impossible* could be playing the day that student teams are doing an experimental exercise. Or "We Are the Champions" by Queen could be the theme when teams make end-of-the-semester presentations.

At the end of each class, a teacher may also ask students to consider that day's experience and what they have learned that is important to them by writing down two or three takeaways. The purpose is to have students walk out of the room continuing to think about and reflect upon their own learning and to consider finding ways to apply that learning going forward.

THE LAST DAY

There is a final chance on the last day of the course for a teacher to apply the mantra *Anything different is good.* A teacher can share personal rules or lessons learned that have guided them in their lives and discipline. They can provide a note to each student wishing them well on their continued journey. They can read and distribute a favorite poem that has special meaning to them and may have a special meaning for the students.

A teacher who promotes creativity in their classroom will try to end their course as they sought to begin it—with students willing to "think different" and learn differently. Maybe after the journey of this course, their students will agree that *anything different is good.* Perhaps they will even add, as Phil the weatherman did, "But this could be real good."

Chapter 6

Say, "Yes, And"

Every day, the unexpected happens. The best-laid plans go awry. Something occurs to take us off course. Those who overcome obstacles, who deal in a positive way with adversity, and who respond creatively to the unanticipated, improvise. In any discipline, career, or position, those who succeed seem to be able to "make things up as they go along." They learn to pivot, change directions, and forge ahead. How can teachers find ways to incorporate the skills and know-how of improvisation in their own teaching?

Four Day Weekend, an improv troupe, performs at their theater in Sundance Square in Fort Worth, Texas. During their show, the performers put on an impressive display of improvisation. They ask audience members to shout out places, propose situations, recommend foods, name celebrities, toss out colors, make up occupations, and suggest roles to play—the more improbable the connections, the more outlandish the pairing, the more ridiculous the suggestions, the better!

On the spot, the actors weave together stories connecting all the dots, make up funny skits around the range of weird offerings, even create situations in which they are able to relate seemingly unrelatable ideas. For one of their acts, they invite an audience member to come up onstage and then interview the person about their life and experience while tossing a football back and forth. Then they create and perform a song that covers all the key activities in that person's life with wit and insight. They dazzle audiences.

No suggestion is too outrageous. No idea is too wild. No situation is too impossible. They respond to each and every proposal with alacrity. They deal with each and every thought with creativity. They address each and every challenge with a can-do attitude.

41

What if teachers, in any discipline, could teach the skills and attitudes of improvisation to their students? How creative could a class be if students were really good at making things up as they went along? How might the philosophy of improvisation be applied to problem solving, critical thinking, the pursuit of opportunity, and the development of creativity in any classroom?

THE "YES, AND" PHILOSOPHY

The foundation of improvisation is the "yes, and" philosophy. The "yes" acknowledges that one recognizes and understands the possibility of what someone else says or proposes. The "and" then contributes something positive and constructive to that possibility.

Two timely books are useful in understanding the "yes, and" philosophy. In *Happy Accidents: The Transformative Power of "Yes, And" at Work and in Life*, David Ahearn, Frank Ford, and David Wilk, founders of Four Day Weekend, demonstrate how "yes, and" can lead to opportunity in any career.[1] Kelly Leonard and Tom Yorton from Second City in Chicago show how "yes, and" can enhance any person's creativity in *Yes, And: How Improvisation Reverses "No, But" Thinking and Improves Creativity and Collaboration*.[2]

The "yes, and" philosophy of improvisation fights the more usual tendency to say, "No, but." There are always reasons to turn down something when it is offered, to refuse a suggestion, to decline an invitation, to ignore an opportunity. One could always argue that there is not enough time, money, or other resources to pursue a new possibility. Or one could maintain that the situation is too uncertain, ambiguous, or risky to pursue.

The ability to think and act creatively, however, in whatever position, career, or discipline in which a person is engaged requires the willingness to be open to possibilities, to avoid initially saying, "No, but," and to give possibilities the chance to flourish. How can a teacher bring that "yes, and" perspective to the courses they teach? How do they help their students learn to say, "Yes, and"? What kinds of insights, activities, and exercises can demonstrate key principles of improvisation?

Say, "Yes, And"

The essential requirement for improvisation to work is the willingness to say, "Yes, and." Teaching thus requires some kind of activity or exercise that encourages unusual suggestions and unconventional connections on the one hand while allowing on the other for affirmation of those suggestions and connections and encouraging new thoughts about and additions to them. One technique to communicate how "yes, and" can work is an exercise called "forced pairs," which was presented at a conference of the United States Association for Small Business and Entrepreneurship during one of its workshops on experiential learning.

In forced pairs, a student makes a list of three items that they love to do. Maybe cooking, sailing, golfing, knitting, sleeping, hunting, or traveling—any three items that they find interesting and fun to do. Then, that student is paired with another student who has also made their three-item list. Together, each student takes their top item and matches it to their partner's top item. Then they match their second items and then their third items. Once they have matched items, they must create a product or service that addresses these new connections. Often, the connections are wildly different . . . and the products and services wonderfully creative.

As the exercise progresses, students say, "Yes" to the connection, as unusual and unconventional as it may be, and then they say, "And" by identifying the possibilities that the match creates. So bicycle riding and cooking leads to a video about preparing a recipe while riding one's exercise bike. Drinking wine and traveling results in a special guided tour of wineries in Italy. Knitting and fly-fishing combine to make customized sweaters with a fishing motif.

During the exercise, students discover possibilities. "No, but" is never mentioned. Not a single student says that a connection is impossible or makes no sense or is too ridiculous to deal with. No one opts to kill an idea or shut down a match. Instead, students affirm their partner's suggestion and then add something new and positive to the match. In other words, students begin to discover the energy and creativity that can come by saying, "Yes, and." (See exhibit 5 in the appendix.)

Listen Actively

A second key attribute of improvisation is active listening. To affirm what someone has said and then to offer something positive as a response requires that one pay full attention to what another is saying and then demonstrate genuine interest in what is said. Active listening requires eliminating distractions, setting aside one's own point of view, and seeking first to understand rather than trying to be understood.

To help students appreciate the importance of listening to successful improvisation, a teacher can conduct a storytelling exercise. In this activity, each student recalls a wonderful experience that they have had. Perhaps it is a trip or a celebration or a concert, but something that they vividly remember because it was so enjoyable. Then, working with a partner, one student is the storyteller and tells their story in one minute, in as much detail as possible to the other, recalling the place, the people, the sights, the smells, the colors, and the sounds, all of which made their experience so memorable. The other student, who is the listener, must pay attention and then tell the story back to the original storyteller with as much accuracy as possible.

The original storyteller then grades the listener from A to F on the listener's ability to get the story right. The students then reverse roles and do the same thing. In almost every case, the listener earns an A for their ability to retell the story effectively. In other words, they pay attention, eliminate distractions, and focus on hearing the details.

This exercise has one additional step. After each student has served as both a storyteller and a listener, they must each recall a second happy and memorable story. But this time, they tell their stories to each other simultaneously. Of course, chaos erupts. Students talk over and past each other, telling their own stories while trying to hear the story of their partner. Listening becomes impossible. Instead of seeking to understand, their priority is to be understood, so they never hear the other's story.

This is a fun, insightful, and convincing exercise about what helps or hinders the ability to listen to another person. In the debrief, the connection to improvisation becomes clear. If one is focused primarily on expressing what is on their mind, whether that is selling a product or service, proving an argument, or trying to convince another of something, then the chances for taking advantage of possibilities are limited. Only by listening carefully can a person understand the needs, problems, and issues of others; fully comprehend the opportunities that may be presented to them; and improvise constructively to respond to the inevitable unexpected changes that will occur around them.

Stay in the Moment

A third critical element of improvisation, related to active listening, is the ability to stay in the moment. Successful improvisation demands staying in the here and now; not jumping ahead with one's own thoughts, suggestions, and ideas; and not trying to anticipate the answers of others or one's own priorities.

The specific talent of those gifted in improvisation is that they are able to be fully alert to what is being said and what is happening in the very moment that it is occurring. Since they don't know what may be coming or what may be said, they don't try to anticipate the future. They remain patient enough and alert enough and comfortable enough to respond to what they have heard and seen in the moment in which they have heard it and seen it. The ability to stay in the moment is a useful skill to learn in whatever discipline in which one is engaged.

There are several techniques to help students learn to stay in the moment. One that can involve an entire class is to have students recount an imaginary trip in the classroom. Each student, when it comes their turn, must add a dimension to the trip that can go anywhere, meet with anybody, and conduct any kind of activity. For example, the teacher may start the trip. Then each one of them must add to the trip when it comes to their turn by building upon what the student before them has just said and adding to it. An example might go like the following.

"I loved our safari," the teacher begins. Going around the room, one student after other adds their possibilities and takes the class in unanticipated directions: And we rode elephants. And the elephants took us to Victoria Falls. And we went over Victoria Falls in barrels. And a guide recorded us and put us on TikTok. And Martin Scorsese saw the video and Hollywood made a movie of us. And we went to the Oscars. . . . And so it goes as each student adds something positive to what has gone before.

This activity combines "yes, and" with active listening and the requirement to stay in the moment. No one knows what the person before them will say, where the trip may take them, or what or whom they might encounter along the way. So no one can anticipate an answer or jump ahead. Each must stay in the moment.

TEACHER AS IMPROV PERFORMER

Improvisation is both an attitude and a behavior. The attitude is the willingness to make things up as one goes along, to embrace the realization that one cannot anticipate everything, and to realize that the unexpected will happen, even in the classroom. The behavior requires that a teacher apply the "yes, and" approach to their interactions with students; listen actively to their concerns, ideas, and suggestions; and stay in the moment in the classroom.

Improvisation influences teaching in practical ways. When students come up with new and interesting ways to approach a project or complete an assignment, a teacher should keep the "yes, and" philosophy in mind. Try to avoid saying, "No, but." Instead, look for ways to implement their ideas and recommendations. As a result, students are always more enthused and committed to do the assignment or to complete the project well.

By understanding the elements of improvisation, a teacher listens much more actively (and watches much more carefully) for the teachable moment. They are more willing to "go with the flow" when the unexpected occurs, to set aside the planned objective for the day, and to shift emphasis when something unanticipated and potentially important emerges. A teacher learns to consciously set aside all other activities, projects, emails, and apparent priorities when a student wants to discuss a problem, share a concern, or seek their advice. They work to stay in the moment with them.

In education today, the ability to improvise has become a critical competency for teachers and students alike in every discipline. By utilizing the skills of improvisation, teachers can help their students learn how to deal with ambiguity and uncertainty, find creative ways to solve problems, and know how to take better advantage of opportunities.

Section II

Creativity and Teaching

Takeaways

Section II on "Creativity and Teaching" has considered ways to make a teacher's classroom more creative, engaging, and spontaneous. It contends that all students are creative and that teachers can help them recognize their creative talents by encouraging a willingness to be wrong, focusing on making unconventional connections, and learning from mistakes.

Teachers can design an environment for creativity and generate the curiosity of their students by focusing on the mantra that *anything different is good* and then applying that approach to the way they communicate and interact with their students.

An essential element of the creative process is to understand and apply the lessons of improvisation to solve problems more innovatively and to take advantage of opportunities more expeditiously.

Think about three takeaways related to your approach to creativity. What struck you as interesting, surprising, and/or applicable to your situation? How would you assess your own creative talents? How do you engender an environment of creativity in your discipline, your classroom, or your laboratory? How important is improvisation in what you do?

Specific takeaways might include: trying one of the creativity exercises in your class, such as half of thirteen or round objects; writing your own precourse invitation or revising your syllabus to make them more personal, engaging, and intriguing; opening one of your classes with music; and utilizing a "yes, and" activity, like the storytelling exercise.

SECTION III

Teaching for Excitement

Chapter 7

Oh, No! A Lecture!

"Oh, no! I have to listen to a lecture? Not a lecture! That's so boring!" Can't you hear your students, or any audience, saying this? The last teaching technique that anyone seems to want as part of their learning experience is to have to sit through a lecture. The experience conjures up the scene in *Ferris Bueller's Day Off* of a teacher droning on, then posing a question and, when no one responds, asking, "Anyone? Anyone?" When no one answers, he then gives the answer himself and proceeds to start the same process all over again.

It does not have to be this way. A lecture can be not only a creative and energizing opportunity for a teacher but also an active, engaging, and enjoyable learning experience for those participating in the event.

Sometimes teachers have knowledge, experience, and even wisdom to share that can only be done through a lecture. So, what makes for a really good lecture, whether one is presenting to the students in their class or standing before a throng waiting to hear what a teacher might say?

THREE KEY QUESTIONS

Every lecture begins with three questions: What does a teacher want the audience to know? What does a teacher want them to feel? What does a teacher want them to do? These are the essential elements of any effective and engaging lecture.

The know-feel-do strategy shapes a teacher's thinking and helps them focus on ways to engage others in the lecture experience.[1] For example, in a presentation on "How to Give a Really Great Lecture," teachers should learn how to prepare for a lecture, how to manage the stage experience, how to present a clear message, and how to make their lecture active and engaging. They should feel excited, motivated, and energized. They should be able to incorporate the lessons learned in their next lecture.

If these areas are addressed effectively, then each person attending will not only have participated in an active learning experience of their own but will also be able to better engage, influence, and interact with their students when they lecture.

GOING ONSTAGE

A lecture is a performance. The teacher is a performer. One does not need to tap-dance in front of the audience or yell and scream or pretend to be something one is not. But an effective teacher does need to be prepared, credible, and genuine.

The first task after considering the three key questions is to make sure that the lecturer *owns the room*. Whether that is one's classroom or a lecture hall or a convention floor, a teacher must own the room in which they are speaking. Owning the room means the teacher is completely familiar with the place in which they speak, eliminates all possible distractions from themselves and their message, and is as comfortable as possible with the space around them.

Often a teacher walks into a classroom in which another teacher or speaker has preceded them. There may be mathematical equations on the board from an algebra course or chemical formulas from a chemistry class or data from a statistics class or notes from a class on Shakespeare. To own the room, clear everything away. Move chairs, tables, and moveable podiums out of the way. Turn off the cell phone. In other words, control as much of the space as possible.

Owning the room helps to reduce anxiety and provides a sense of mastery over the environment. In fact, even when committing to a lecture in a new location, a smart lecturer will ask about how the room is arranged, how the audience will be seated, what audiovisual equipment might be available, where the exits are located, whether the podium is moveable, whether there will be a head table and, if so, who will be seated at it. A lecturer should get as clear a picture as possible of the place where they will be lecturing so that they know what to expect even before they get there.

In a real sense, a lecture is an event, like going to a concert or taking in a play or participating in an enjoyable celebration, like a wedding or a birthday. Viewing a lecture like an event requires a different kind of mindset about what a lecture should be. Rather than something tedious, lecture-as-event implies something energizing, memorable, and even joyous.

Consider what makes an event memorable? There are two important elements that are also present with a lecture. First, an event is a gathering of like-minded people. They are all there for a similar reason: they like the concert performer or they know the wedding couple's families or they share an appreciation for the activity, whatever it might be. Those attending a lecture are there because they have chosen to come because they have something in common about the topic or the class. This gathering of the like-minded suggests that students have a need or desire to participate in the presentation.

Second, an event provides a sense of community for those involved. John Gardner was an advisor to presidents, a winner of the Medal of Freedom, a distinguished teacher, and a noted author. In his important publication *Building Community*, he highlights the essential elements for people to feel a sense of togetherness: identity (that the event reflects who they are and what they value), belonging (that it provides a belief that one should be part of a larger group), and security (that the event is a safe place to be).[2] When all three are present, such as in a classroom during a lecture, then participants feel a sense of community, which in turn makes the teacher-as-lecturer and those who listen to the lecture part of the same community.

This combination of a gathering of like-minded with a sense of community provides a wonderful opportunity for human interaction, which is essential in a classroom and necessary for learning.

Think for a moment about two lectures that you have personally attended. It's important to think of two that you actually sat through. Recall one that was really terrific, that you thoroughly enjoyed, that didn't just inform but also inspired you. Remember another that was terrible, that you couldn't wait to leave, that left you disappointed and frustrated.

In comparing these, the factors that make one lecture fantastic and the other a disaster become apparent. The terrific lecture no doubt was surprising, engaging, interesting. The speaker was thoughtful, informed, open, and maybe even self-deprecating, changed the level of their voice, had good eye contact, and was interested in their own topic. The disastrous lecture was dull, full of jargon, difficult to comprehend, and boring. The speaker seemed uninspired, spoke in a monotone, read the slides on the screen, and seemed to wish to be somewhere else.

In their wonderful book *Made to Stick*, Chip and Dan Heath present a powerful model for why some ideas stick in our minds and others don't.[3] Their SUCCESs model is also key to understanding why one lecture can be terrific and another can be a disaster. They contend that for something, like a lecture, to stick powerfully in our mind certain factors must be addressed:

- The lecture must be S (simple). It must capture in clear and understandable terms the essence of the message. No jargon or speaking over the heads of others or convoluted messaging.
- It must be U (unexpected). It has to violate our expectations in some way and surprise us.
- It must be C (concrete). It has to provide vivid images that others can see, sense, and feel in some way.
- It must be C (credible). It should come across as honest, believable, and genuine.
- It must be E (emotional). It should call on the emotions of others and not just their intellects.
- It must tell Ss (stories). While data, statistics, and various forms of evidence are important, a good story leaves a lasting impression.

By following these guidelines, two lectures, with dramatically different styles, can leave lasting impressions. Sir Ken Robinson lectured on creativity to an audience of about a thousand. He stood on a raised platform and talked for about an hour and fifteen minutes. No slides, no PowerPoint, no exhibits. He just talked. And he was spellbinding.

Jim Hayhurst was a member of a Canadian expedition to climb Mount Everest and wrote a remarkable book about the experience, *The Right Mountain*.[4] He used a set of slides in a lecture to show the attempt on the summit, which ultimately failed. In recounting the effort, he raised critical questions, like "What is success?" and "What values guide us?" He had the full and undivided attention of everyone who heard him. Lectures like these are memorable learning experiences. The lecturer is clearly and deeply interested in the topic about which they speak. Their genuine interest is contagious. After all, if the lecturer is not really involved and interested in their topic, why should anyone else be?

Effective lecturers are credible. They find ways to communicate their credibility to their audience with three approaches:

- *Inference.* Even though one may have never met or heard of the lecturer, one may infer that the speaker is credible given their experience, credentials, publications, and awards.
- *Reference.* What others say about a person is important. Thus, a testimonial from someone who introduces the lecturer saying good things about them adds to their credibility.
- *Evidence.* The final and most important determination of credibility is proof. If, after hearing a lecture, listeners have found useful insights, practical recommendations, and specific ideas that they can readily apply, then the speaker's credibility goes up. (And if not, then credibility goes down.)[5]

The last advantage that a lecturer has is preparation. Appearing to look effortless in giving a lecture actually requires a great deal of time, practice, and know-how. That effortless effect only comes with detailed and informed self-assessment and plain hard work. An accomplished lecturer will spend significant time going over their notes, anticipating questions, considering the needs of the audience, and practicing key parts of what they want to say, even though they may have given the lecture many times before. The result is a lecture that keeps the attention of everyone attending, inspires while it informs, and engages each person in a memorable and creative learning experience.

THE BUTTERFLY EFFECT

Good lecturers still get nervous before they lecture. Even though they may have given a lecture several times before, they still want the one they are doing at the moment to be fresh and meaningful for the students they are teaching. Consequently, it is not unusual for a speaker to experience "butterflies in the stomach." It's that queasy feeling that seems like an upset stomach. Other signs of this condition are a dry mouth and moist hands. In other words, they feel anxious. This is related to the fight-or-flight reaction that prehistoric man encountered when unexpectedly confronting a saber-toothed tiger.

This butterfly effect is actually the release of adrenaline, which occurs whenever a person faces something unexpected and worrisome. Adrenaline is a wonderful natural drug. It sharpens all our senses. One sees better, smells more clearly, hears more sharply. With adrenaline, a person runs faster, jumps higher, becomes stronger. If they can manage the adrenaline, then they can perform better. The key is not to eliminate the butterflies, but to make them fly in formation.

Most performing artists will admit to a case of the butterflies before they go before an audience. They call it stage fright. They want to perform well, and, given their high expectations, they feel nervous as they are about to begin their performance.

There are four practical ways to make sure the butterflies fly in formation.

First, focus on the audience. Some speech teachers dole out bad advice about dealing with nervousness. They maintain that to minimize nervousness, the speaker should ignore the audience or separate them from the reality of the current situation. So they may tell a speaker to imagine they are looking at a clock high on a wall in the back of the room or auditorium, above the heads of their students or audience, to avoid making any eye contact with anyone.

Those in the audience, however, then start looking behind them wondering what in the world the speaker is looking at. Worse, other speech instructors may tell a lecturer to imagine everyone in the audience naked. What!? Don't go there! All of this is terrible advice. In fact, just the opposite is key to helping to manage nervousness.

Before a lecture, the accomplished lecturer makes it a point to meet members of the audience, shake some hands, and introduce themselves personally. In other words, they establish a meaningful connection with students or audience members before the lecture even begins. Then they purposely look for someone in the audience who will smile back at them.

There is always the person who sits with folded arms with a frown on their face, staring back at a lecturer as if to say, "I'm going to make this hard for you." Good lecturers don't look at that person. Most of those waiting to hear a lecture really want the lecturer to do well and are actually cheering for the person to impress them.

Second, visualize the lecture. Before beginning actually talking, a prepared lecturer walks through the entire lecture in their mind. They see themselves stepping out onstage, clapping with the audience at their introduction, hearing their opening words, running through their visual aids if using any, giving their talk, and hearing the final applause. In this way, the actual process of giving a lecture is something that a speaker has already done mentally. In this way, they are making the butterflies fly in formation.

Third, practice. A speaker can reduce the novelty and uncertainty of an experience—that which causes the nervousness—with practice. The more opportunities to accept to lecture, the better a teacher can get at it. Practice lets a person test what works and what may not. It provides immediate feedback on ways to hone a message and identify the most salient points. It provides an avenue to respond to audience questions. It allows the speaker to better understand and develop their own style.

Fourth, label the experience differently. Perhaps most important, a teacher should label the experience of giving a lecture in more positive terms. Because people are worried about failing or looking stupid or appearing silly, they fear giving a talk more than death! But much of that fear is self-imposed. A person thinks that giving a lecture is an awful experience, so they feel terrible that they have to do it, and thus they perform poorly. This think-feel-act mentality works against them rather than for them.

Instead, an effective lecturer tells themselves that giving a lecture is a truly wonderful chance to share their experience, improve an important skill, and engage others in a creative way. Feeling more positive about the lecture experience results in a better performance.

Consider whether a person likes or hates riding a roller coaster. Those who like the ride rush to the front of the line so that they can run to the front car. As the coaster clicks its way up the first hill, they raise their arms and shout, "Hands free!" As the ride proceeds, they yell and even scream the whole time. When the coaster arrives back at the starting point, they want to do it all over again.

The person who hates a roller coaster avoids the front car. They go to the car in the middle of the coaster, scrunch over, grab the bar with white knuckles, never look up, and then yell and even scream for the whole ride. When they get back to the start, they decide never to do it again. Why is one ride exhilarating and the other exhausting? Part of the reason is how a person labels the experience.

A lecturer can manage the butterflies one other way even with good visual aids. Often a speaker puts up a PowerPoint slide or a graphic of some kind that is indecipherable to an audience—dense, wordy, complicated. Then the speaker will even tell the audience, "I know you can't read this!" Or "I know this is too confusing to understand." Given the technical capabilities of PowerPoint today, too may lecturers fall into the trap of "death by PowerPoint."

Speakers do this because the slide or graphic is not a visual aid for their students or audience but a visual dependency for them. They fear they will give a poor talk if they don't have the slide or graphic to remind them of each and every thing to say. So a speaker will use a visual dependency to read directly from the slide or graphic or to remind themselves of what they should be talking about.

A few years ago, a major international business plan competition brought together teams from some of the leading business schools in the world to pitch their plans to a distinguished group of venture capitalists, successful private investors, and renowned entrepreneurs. One team from a famous school used a PowerPoint presentation in which they literally read what was on each slide. About eight minutes into their twenty-minute presentation, the computer stopped working for some reason. Their presentation came to an embarrassing halt. They could not give their pitch without their dependence on the slides.

That afternoon, another team from a renowned business school was in the midst of their presentation when the computer collapsed again. The two students on the team did not miss a beat. The stepped down from the stage, stood before the judges, and said, "Let us tell you about our plan." They dazzled the judges and the audience. Their aids were actually aids, not dependencies. They did not need them to give their presentation.

Every time that a teacher steps before their students or another audience to deliver a lecture, they should anticipate that their PowerPoint or other visual aids (if they are using them) will fail, and that they will be expected to give their talk without them.

Visual aids can be wonderful additions to a lecture, but only if they truly aid students and the audience in enjoying the lecture. This means keeping the aids brief, concise, easy to read, understandable, and supportive of the point that the lecturer is making. There is a surefire guide to determining whether a slide meets these guidelines. Follow the 6x6 rule: no more than six lines on a slide with no more than six words per line. Then put the slide on the floor, stand up, and look at it. If it is clearly and easily readable, then it's a good visual aid. If not, then it needs to be redone.

THE WOW FACTOR

Every effective lecture leaves an audience saying, "Wow! I'm glad I attended!" What can a teacher do to help make sure that every person in their class or in the audience has a wow experience? This requires a teacher to use structure, demonstration, and the application of active learning strategies.

Anyone who has camped knows what it is like to set up a tent. Campers begin with a center pole to raise the tent and then utilize four additional poles, one at each corner, to secure the tent. In planning a lecture, a teacher should set up their speaking tent. Establish one essential point to make, and then identify three or four key supporting points (the poles for the corners of their tent) that they want to emphasize (own the room, going onstage, the butterfly effect, and the wow factor). A lecturer can remember three or four key points. They can't remember fifteen or twenty. The center pole and four corner poles provide the structure for the lecture.

One of the most important secrets to a really great lecture is to be highly redundant during the lecture. Repetition, which is saying the same thing in the same way over and over again, is tedious and boring. Saying the same thing in many different ways is being redundant and is interesting and captivating for an audience.

Redundancy is an engaging way to keep the attention of your students and reinforce key points. An effective lecturer will tell a story (the experience of the two business school teams); tie in a book (*The Right*

Mountain); mention a movie scene (*Ferris Bueller*); give an example (the tent strategy); provide an analogy (roller coasters); or supply a personal example, an interesting statistic, a humorous anecdote, or a telling demonstration. This kind of variety enriches a lecture and engages the audience.

Redundancy has one other advantage for the teacher. It allows the speaker to have an "accordion" ability to fit their lecture into any required time frame. A speaker can expand or constrict their lecture like opening or closing an accordion. For example, if one has only ten minutes on a panel to speak, they just mention their four key points without going into any detail. If they have thirty minutes, they will mention each of the four points and then add a supporting comment or two. If they have two hours, then they can utilize their entire panoply of redundancy options around their key points. It is the same talk each time, but redundancy allows a speaker to fit it into any time frame.

Wow also comes by incorporating active learning strategies into the lecture. A lecture can seem like a one-way form of communication. The lecturer talks, and students or those in the audience listen. Not so! A great lecture requires interaction and participation. Each person attending should be involved and engaged. For this to happen, the lecturer has to include ways to involve and engage them. It's actually easy to do.

The most basic of active learning strategies is to simply ask questions. For larger audiences, a speaker can ask people to raise their hands in response to a question. For classes of students, a teacher can seek responses to questions. Importantly, the more personalized the question, the more engaged the audience becomes. For example, instead of asking, "What makes for a good lecture and a bad lecture?" Ask instead, "Think of a lecture that you really liked and one that you really hated. What makes one excellent and the other a disappointment?"

By personalizing a question, a lecturer invokes not just memory among attendees but also emotion. That emotion engages an audience. No matter the topic, questions that get attendees to recall a personal experience are intrinsically engaging. Instead of asking, for illustration, "What factors make for a successful team?" Ask, "Think about teams that you were on. Why were some great and why were others terrible?" The goal is to have attendees respond emotionally and not just intellectually.

Short writes are a powerful way for students or audience members to actually reflect on their own learning while listening to and interacting with a lecture. Before transitioning to another tent pole or theme in their talk, a speaker may have the audience take two minutes and write down three things that they have found interesting, surprising, or useful that they would like to reflect on further. In this way, each one listening takes away from that portion of the lecture something personal to them. If there is time, a speaker can ask some to share their reflections.

Each person brings their own background, experience, and current issues into their short writes. This is much more effective and enjoyable for students and audiences than trying to take notes, which are essentially a summary of what the lecturer is talking about. An engaging lecture has students tie their own experience to the topic at hand. At the end of a lecture, participants can write down their three takeaways so that they have things to think about after the talk.

Finally, a teacher can have students learn from each other during a lecture. Students can pair up with a person next to them for two or three minutes to discuss an issue. Or, groups of four or five students can share their experiences on a topic. An adept lecturer may even require attendees to have a kinetic experience by moving their bodies, turning around to face others, changing the position of their chairs, stretching to see and hear others. This kind of variety is often unexpected but always welcomed as a way to inject spontaneity, participation, and involvement in a lecture.

For a teacher, it is a privilege to have the opportunity to deliver a lecture to their classes or to other audiences. By combining the personal, the engaging, and the surprising, giving a lecture can be a creative teaching act that results in a meaningful learning experience.

Chapter 8

Experience Onstage

A guest speaker can be a wonderful addition to a class. Their been-there, done-that experience, their thoughtful reflection, and their energy and enthusiasm can enrich a learning experience. Or their arrogance, condescension, and boorish behavior can make for an unmitigated disaster.

Finding and using guest speakers would seem to be a piece of cake for a teacher. Just call them up, invite them to come to class, and then let them talk. Easy, peasy, right? Not so fast! For some teachers, there can also be a certain measure of laziness attached to inviting a guest speaker to their classes. During a busy semester, having a guest speaker might allow a teacher to coast through a class or two so that they can focus on research that they might be doing at the time.

It seems like a no-brainer for a teacher to invite a prominent person in their discipline to come and speak to their class. Just call them up, invite them to tell their story, and then expect to hear an insightful and inspirational account of their experience. If the speaker bombs by criticizing the class, talking down to the students, and praising their own accomplishments, it is easy to blame the speaker for an awful presentation. That is, until the teacher realizes that the fault is not with the speaker but with themselves. The teacher never took the time to get to know the speaker, never tried to learn their story and how it might complement the course, and ignored preparing the speaker and their students for the presentation.

As a result, using outside guest speakers to try to enrich a class tends to be a hit-and-miss phenomenon in teaching. Some speakers do well. Others disappoint. Consequently, teachers need to rethink their whole approach on how to incorporate the experience of outside speakers into their courses or simply not use them at all.

THE PLAY'S THE THING

Shakespeare noted, "The play's the thing." A good play can not only catch the conscience of a king as it does in *Hamlet*, but it can also enliven a learning experience. However, for guest speakers to have genuine impact on a class, a teacher must reimagine their role in the course and envision a different way to include guest speakers in classes.

To achieve this, a teacher must take on the role of a movie or Broadway director. Their classroom is the stage, and their course is their movie or Broadway production. A class becomes a scene in their movie or play, with each class or scene building on the preceding one, all leading up to the denouement or climax of the course. As the director, it is the teacher's responsibility to ensure that their course is Oscar worthy or a Tony Award winner. That includes making sure that everyone who appears in their production is selected carefully, has rehearsed thoroughly, and performs effectively.

Teachers seek to provide as rewarding a learning experience as possible for their students. When an outside speaker is cast appropriately, they can contribute to an exciting and memorable teaching moment. A guest speaker's role in the course script can be important and impactful when they:

- *Provide a reality check.* Outside speakers bring real-world and real-time knowledge that complements and extends the traditional academic environment. Their personal experience helps to make lessons come alive and gives students the opportunity to gain practical know-how.
- *Reinforce messages.* By talking about what works and what does not, outside speakers reinforce key points that a textbook or readings may make and supports a teacher's own instruction. Their stories are an additional way to communicate strategies, tactics, approaches, and issues that are under discussion in the class.
- *Add pizzazz.* Outside speakers, especially those who are more well known regionally and nationally, add excitement to the learning process. Because their reputations precede them, they help to spark interest in the topic at hand and build enthusiasm for the course.
- *Inspire.* Outside speakers are role models. They provide living proof that obstacles can be overcome, that challenges can be met,

and that creativity and innovation are possible. They serve to motivate students. In the best cases, they demonstrate how values and ethics are an essential part of success in any field of endeavor.

CASTING FOR THE PART

To ensure that a speaker meets the objectives of a class, a teacher must prepare both the guest speaker and their students. A teacher should personally meet the guest speaker, learn about their story, and understand how it might relate to their class. The teacher needs to prepare the guest speaker for the session by telling them what to expect with the students. At the same time, it is critical to prepare the students for the experience by explaining to them who the guest speaker is and why they have been invited to the class. In other words, in their role as a director, a teacher has to develop a way to cast potential outside speakers for the part that they would play in the production of their course.

The teacher-as-director starts by identifying potential cast members. Through their own contacts and the contacts of others, by tapping the alumni network of the school and various organizations in their discipline, by interacting with people in the community, and through connecting with a range of institutions supporting programs in their college, a teacher can develop a long list of promising speakers. The challenge then is to narrow down their casting search based on a number of criteria:

- *Fit with the course and topic.* Critically, the experience of the speaker must fit the subject of a particular class. By having coffee or lunch with the person, visiting their operation, and learning their story, a teacher can better recognize the specific value added that they could bring to the topic under discussion in their course.
- *Ability to relate to their students.* Speakers who are open and candid with a teacher are likely to be open and candid with students. Promising speakers ask about the purpose of the class, the demographics of the students, and what they might bring to a memorable learning experience, not only for the students but also for themselves. Effective guest speakers communicate a sense of

excitement about the possibility of interacting with bright, energetic, and creative students.

- *Talent to tell a compelling story.* Peter Drucker, one of the most influential management experts of the twentieth century, made a telling comment about the educational process: "To enhance a learning experience, tell a compelling story."[1] By that he meant that, while data, statistics, and theory are important, it is the compelling story that communicates memorably how to overcome adversity, how to innovate, how to make a difference. In casting for a part, the teacher-as-director listens to how a potential speaker tells their story to them.
- *Willingness to reflect on their own learning.* An effective outside speaker has thought carefully about their experience, has reflected on the lessons they have learned, and is honest about both their successes and their failures. Importantly, they are willing to share this reflection and their learning with others.

One of the intriguing issues for a speaker in any field is not what they have learned from their successes but what they have learned from their failures. This requires honest self-awareness and candid self-reflection. It is sometimes hard to find someone willing to speak openly about the mistakes they have made and the failures they have encountered. But those who do provide an especially dramatic and memorable learning experience for students.

THE REHEARSAL

Just as actors in a play or a movie will try out for a part, so too do speakers try out for their roles in a teacher's production. Once they get the part, then the real work begins as they come to more fully understand their role, identify their unique approach to the part, and prepare for their performance. As the director, a teacher helps them understand the context of the scene, the vision for their performance, and the goal of the specific class in which they will appear.

To plan the rehearsal, a teacher should do the following:

- *First, set the scene.* The teacher-as-director needs to explain the nature of the audience and describe to whom the speaker will be presenting. They provide the syllabus, which is the storyboard for the play; provide demographics on the makeup of the students; outline what is expected to happen during their scene or visit to the classroom; and clearly delineate how the teacher envisions their specific role.
- *Second, review the script.* The teacher then identifies key points on which they would like the speaker to focus. They review what the speaker can contribute to the topic at hand and explain the goals of the specific class in which they are featured. By providing general guidelines to highlight key learning lessons from them, the teacher can work with them to identify the important takeaways from their talk that students should be able to reflect upon.
- *Third, identify the part.* The teacher and the speaker should both agree on the part that the speaker should play. A speaker could be the guest in a talk show format in which the teacher asks questions, which are prepared after understanding the speaker's experience and determining the format in which they will be most comfortable. The setting is like a late night talk show or like the environment of the Actors Studio. A variation on this is to have a panel of two to three entrepreneurs who interact with one another in responding to the teacher's interview questions. This approach lets the teacher control the discussion and focus on their key learning goals.

  The speaker could be the single storyteller with a monologue that weaves their tale around issues that have been jointly identified. The speaker could be a surprise commentator after a case study discussion revolving around key decisions that arise in the case. In another type of surprise, the speaker could appear to be a visitor who participates in the class revolving around themes that have been important to their experience. The speaker could even present a case study of their own. The goal is to make sure that the speaker becomes a starring attraction in the teacher's learning production.

No matter the role, as the director, a teacher must make clear to every outside speaker what their role will be. It is up to the teacher to emphasize what they want to accomplish and what they expect of the speaker. It is also the teacher's right, as the director, to interject their comments during the presentation to help a speaker keep on track. Then, the teacher should put all of this in writing in an email or memo to the guest speaker ahead of time. In that way, once a teacher says, "Action," no actor in their play is surprised if and when the teacher jumps in to keep the focus of their performance on the goals set for the class. (See exhibit 6 in the appendix.)

THE BEST AND THE WORST PERFORMERS

Outside speakers who are disasters in the classroom demonstrate some common failings:

- *They come unprepared.* Poor performers don't put the time and effort into their presentations, are unfamiliar with the purpose of the course or the specific topic of the class, and show little or no personal reflection on their own experience. Like an old codger, they simply tell their own war stories. The result is the worst of all possible outcomes—they come across as boring and arrogant.
- *They ignore the audience.* Poor speakers, who have ignored focusing on the nature of their audience, talk down to students. They don't appreciate how savvy today's students actually are. Instead of interacting with them, they dictate, like a general giving orders to their troops. They ignore questions and then rush out at the end of class. The clear message that they convey is that their performance is not a priority with them and that they would rather be somewhere else.
- *They pontificate.* Presentations turn into disasters when speakers become so "I" focused that their own arrogance overwhelms any message they are trying to convey. Instead of using their talk as a learning experience, disappointing speakers are prima donnas. They brag about their own credentials, try to tell the students how to live their lives, drop names in an attempt to make themselves look important, and play up their own exploits.
- *They run amok on time.* The worst performers show disdain for the time constraints of their scene. They get off message, take up

far more class time than they are allocated, and try to monopolize the stage.

The best outside speakers provide not only information but also inspiration. They convey not just practical knowledge but also wisdom. They serve not only as experts in their fields but more importantly as role models in their disciplines. They do all this because:

- *They connect with students.* Good performers bring a thoughtful, analytical perspective to the real-life experience they offer. They demonstrate that they have reflected on what they have been through and have learned from that. They are not prescriptive. Rather than tell students what to do, they promote critical thinking by interacting with them to help them come to their own conclusions.
- *They speak truthfully.* In talking about their experience and themselves, effective presenters are honest about what happened and the impact it has had on them. They talk without pretense about the bad as well as the good. They speak from the heart as well as the head.
- *They show concern for students.* By being attentive to the topic and the course and by seeking the opinions of students during their presentation, effective outside speakers demonstrate that they want to learn as well as teach. They come to class having thought about the makeup of the students, including their backgrounds and expectations. They may even prepare handouts, stay after class to meet students more personally, or provide contact information for students who would like to follow up with them later.

Some of the most meaningful and memorable learning experiences can come from faculty in a range of disciplines. A professor in the College of Fine Arts, who may be an actor, director, musician, or composer, can conduct a class on imagineering—the ability to think outside the proverbial box. That professor might put students into a range of different theatrical roles, like writer, performer, stage manager, producer, marketer, and so on. And then have students develop and produce their own play, all within an hour and twenty minutes.

A teacher can take their class to another teacher's classroom to learn about dealing with ambiguity. A classical dance professor can have business students write their names with their bodies using movements from classical dance for a mind-bending and thoroughly entertaining exposure to the process of thinking and learning completely differently than what they are used to.

APPLAUDING THE PERFORMANCE

Following up the performance of the outside guest speaker is critically important. A teacher should debrief their students' encounter to assess what they have learned and conduct a class discussion of lessons learned focusing on what was interesting, unexpected, and potentially useful from a speaker's performance. Students can write a one-page, single-spaced "experience memo." The memo is a thoughtful and focused assessment of what they have learned and how they will incorporate their learning into their personal and professional lives.

The teacher-as-director makes sure to applaud the performer in their play or movie. They follow up with the outside speaker by sending a handwritten note (no email) to thank them for taking the time and effort to bring their experience to their classroom. They provide a gift like a pen or travel mug or other memento from their school. They make sure to send them a few of the experience memos of the students. Speakers love to read about the impact that they have had and what students may have learned from them.

A great performance in the classroom by an outside speaker can and should spark interest, generate enthusiasm, and energize action. When a speaker enters a class, they have the opportunity to add value to the learning process, share their best knowledge and experience, and make a positive difference in the lives of others. As the director of this production, it is a teacher's responsibility to prepare them to do that.

Witnessing a great performance is an extraordinarily satisfying and rewarding learning experience for both the teacher and their students. Just as important, when an outside speaker seeks not only to teach but also to learn, then the fire of the learning process can burn within them as well.

Chapter 9

Always Know Where Your Head Is At

Experience can be a fast and good teacher.

Anyone who has gone rafting knows the power of a white-water rafting experience. After strapping on life vests and hard hats, rafters set off on an inflated rubber raft. Three rafters man the right side of the raft with paddles in hand while another threesome handles the left side. Strapped into an elevated seat with a backrest in the back of the raft, the guide maneuvers a nine-foot oar in each hand.

As they set off in calm water, the guide practices directions with the rafters to help the rafters navigate the raft before they hit rapids. "Right side paddle," the guide shouts. Then, "Left side paddle," the guide yells. Back and forth the guide goes to help the group get ready for the white water ahead.

Once the raft hits the rapids, the rafters are off on a tumultuous and exhilarating ride over some raging white water. They whoop and holler as they rock and roll over currents that toss them like flotsam. To miss boulders in the river, compensate for dips and turns, and avoid overturning, the guide expertly works the oars while keeping up a steady set of commands: "Right side paddle." "Left side paddle." And down the river they catapult.

At a critical juncture of the trip, they may come upon an obstacle like a pedestrian bridge stretched across the river. Because the water is so high, there is little room between the white caps and the steel undergirders of the bridge. The guide tells the rafters to hunker down while unstrapping the seat belt, folding down the backrest, and nestling low in the back of the raft. Then the guide yells, "Always know where your head is at." As the paddlers bolt under the bridge, they all know where their heads are at. That's when the guide proves to be not only a competent river rafter but a wise one as well. As the raft passes under one more pedestrian bridge on the trip, everyone knows exactly what to do. Experience has taught them.

A teacher is like the guide on a river rafting trip who uses the power of experience in their classes. Students learn by doing. In a real sense, experiential learning is the process about knowing where one's head is at. A teacher should want their students to know where their heads are at so that when they encounter similar situations in whatever career they choose, they already have some sense of what to do; are better prepared for the unexpected; and see experience, whether good or bad, as a valuable learning opportunity.

Unfortunately, many teachers are not aware of the value of experiential learning, do not know how to develop an experiential exercise, and have no idea what their students are supposed to learn from an experience.

To ensure a more meaningful and memorable experience for their students, teachers need to take a different approach and integrate experiential learning into their classes. This requires a structured approach to developing and conducting learning experiences in their courses. Any classroom experience must encompass four elements:

- There must be a clear learning purpose to the experience.
- The experience must fully engage the students.
- There must be an effective debriefing of the experience.
- There must be a useful and immediate application of the experience for the students.

THE PURPOSE

Why do an experiential exercise? What should a teacher want their students to learn by doing? How does a specific experience expand a student's understanding of a specific topic in a specific class? How does that exercise convey something important about the overall goal of a teacher's course? If a teacher doesn't have a clear and cogent answer to these questions, then they should not do an experiential exercise. If they can answer these questions effectively to themselves, then an exercise can prove to be a powerful learning experience.

Consider the classroom experience of the "bag résumé." A traditional résumé is a piece of paper that describes one's work history and presents a person's skills, knowledge, and areas of expertise. But no one is ever hired solely on the basis of a piece of paper. Every interview of a job candidate in any discipline seeks to discover what drives a person; what activities, events, and people helped mold the individual; and what life experiences shaped their personalities.

The bag résumé provides an interactive learning experience to better understand what has shaped and what continues to influence how a person behaves. A teacher can use it to begin a course because the act of presenting one's bag résumé fulfills three purposes at the start of a course: it demonstrates creativity, requires an element of risk taking, and builds an esprit de corps in the class.

The concept is simple. The experience combines a brown paper grocery bag with concrete objects that represent what has most influenced the development of an individual. Instead of writing down credentials, awards, and skills on a piece of paper, the teacher and each student must select objects to put in a grocery bag and then explain in two minutes the meaning of those objects to them.

The exercise is illuminating. By combining the brown bag with personal objects, the exercise demonstrates bisociation, which is essential to creativity. Bisociation is the ability to combine or connect two radically different concepts to come up with something new. When students combine an object with a key influence in their lives, they discover a novel (i.e., creative) way to explain to others who they really are.

The selection of the objects also requires a willingness to take a risk. By candidly showing an object that has been important in shaping one's personality, a student must also be willing to consider something very personal or expose a vulnerability. That takes some courage.

The result is that students gain a new and different appreciation of their classmates. They learn insights that never appear on a piece of paper. They identify others whom they would like to work with on team projects. They gain an understanding of the uniqueness of others.

To help them with the exercise, the teacher must set the example. On the first day of class as a way of introduction, a teacher can present their own bag résumé. Possible objects for a teacher could be the following:

- A photo of themselves as a child. This allows the teacher to explain their roots and mention an important influence or two that shaped them growing up.
- A symbol of a vulnerability. This object could represent an obstacle overcome, a challenge the teacher has faced, a difficult period in their life, or an adversity that has taught the teacher a valuable lesson.
- A university memento. Something from their college or university experience permits the teacher to discuss the impact of their own education and how they took advantage of an opportunity.
- A picture of their current family. The photo allows the teacher to comment on the importance of their spouse and children in shaping their own approach to life and teaching.
- An important book (perhaps one of their own). The teacher can use this to emphasize how their discipline and this class became a calling and not just a job or career.
- A meaningful remembrance. This could include a gift from a key person in the teacher's life, a prized possession that explains their goals and aspirations, or a document that holds special meaning for the teacher.

The teacher then gives each student a brown paper grocery bag. Their assignment for the next class is to come prepared to share their own stories with their own objects with the rest of the class. Student presentations are often stunning and profound.

For example, a student reads a rejection letter from a college to which they had applied and explains how it has driven them to succeed. Another student brings a shovel and tells the class that they used it to dig their own father's grave to lay him to rest as a tribute to him for his love and guidance. Others bring family bibles and explain the importance of their faith, or various kinds of athletic equipment that shaped their personality, or revealing keepsakes left by loving friends and family who have passed away.

In other words, the bag résumé exercise becomes an act of creativity that encourages some risk taking and builds respect, inclusiveness, and unexpected connections among those in the class. (See exhibit 7 in the appendix.)

THE EXERCISE

Once there is a purposeful activity that is integrated with the course and reflects specific learning objectives for a class session, then two other elements are required to make an experience a valuable learning endeavor. The experience must include direct, hands-on participation for everyone in the class. No one sits on the sidelines. No one is just an observer. Rather, each student becomes personally, actively engaged. The other ingredient is harder to ensure but important: a positive attitude from each student. The teacher sets the expectation for this in the first class after their own bag résumé presentation by emphasizing the importance of and the expectation for a positive attitude. A teacher can also tell students that they grade "class contribution" by combining the quality of their oral participation with their active and supportive participation in class exercises. That helps.

What really ensures a good spirit among the group is the genuinely positive attitudes that most students demonstrate from the very beginning that becomes contagious for all in the class. Students begin to relish the opportunity to learn from experiential exercises and look forward to classes that include them. The hands-on dimension and the impact of others on the group are evident in another exercise: the "jazz session."[1]

Improvisation is important in any discipline. How can teachers help students deal with uncertainty and ambiguity? What happens when plans fail? What do we do when the unexpected occurs? We improvise. We change the conditions in which we find ourselves. We collaborate with others. The jazz session helps students address each of these purposes.

Of all acts of improvisation, perhaps jazz is the most spontaneous and original. To make up something in the face of the unexpected is a critical skill in any endeavor. To demonstrate that, in this experiential exercise, students must create an original music composition in fifteen minutes. "What!" some say. "That's impossible. I'm not a musician." Nevertheless, in groups of six to nine members, students must create an original composition and then perform it in front of the class for a full two minutes. If available, a teacher can supply a box full of various instruments like cymbals, triangles, drums, bells, whistles, and flutes. But students can use anything as an instrument, and do, like books, bottles, trash cans, tabletops, and even clicking their own fingers.

The result can be rather dazzling.

Each group develops its own beat, cadence, and rhythm. They discover that in the midst of uncertainty something enjoyable and entertaining can emerge. In just fifteen minutes of practice, they have improvised and discovered that they may be musicians to some degree after all. While they perform, many will use dance and singing to enhance their stage presentation.

During the actual performance, some students will improvise on the spur of the moment to fulfill the two-minute time requirement. So there is improvisation within the improvisation. Every student is active and engaged. Remarkably, they inspire each other to participate with a positive attitude, all of which helps to promote an insightful and memorable learning experience. (See exhibit 8 in the appendix.)

THE DEBRIEF

It's one thing to develop and implement an experiential learning activity. It's another to actually learn from it. Unless one proactively and consciously reflects on a learning experience and then applies the lessons that one takes away from it, then the learning is fleeting, and key lessons that one might take away from an experience fade away. To actually know where one's head is at takes a thoughtful, structured, and candid debrief of the experience. Usually, students on their own don't take the time and effort to do an effective debrief. So, the teacher must make sure that they do.

The debrief of an experiential learning activity involves three steps, each one increasingly detailed, specific, and applicable to a student's particular situation. Since every student brings their own background, issues, knowledge, and past successes and failures to an experiential exercise, each one also takes away unique and personal lessons from that experience. It is the teacher's responsibility to help them understand what they have learned and then apply that learning to their own situation and learning objectives.

The first step in the debrief is to discuss as a class what the students have just gone through in an experiential exercise. This initial review and assessment raises key questions, challenges assumptions, and allows students to share their own perspectives on what just occurred.

For example, the bag résumé raises questions such as "What is creativity?" "What is the power of a good story?" "How should one define oneself?" "What is really important in one's development?" "What is involved in risk taking?" "How can one build an esprit de corps in a team?"

In the jazz session exercise, key questions focus on "What does it mean to improvise?" "How does one feel about and deal with ambiguity?" "What are factors that contribute to or hinder effective communication?" "How does the behavior of one person affect the behavior of others?" "What is required for effective collaboration?"

The initial class review and assessment opens new ways of thinking about an exercise and begins to help students identify lessons that they think are important for them.

The second step goes further in honing what a student takes away from an experiential learning opportunity. Each student writes down three lessons from their involvement in the experience that they believe are interesting, surprising, or useful and that they would like to reflect upon further. This individual reflection requires students to delve a bit deeper into what the experience means to them. Students then share one of their personal takeaways, which highlights the range of lessons that can emerge in an engaging classroom experience.

The last step is to internalize the learning. This happens through an *experience memo*. This is a required and graded assignment with a rubric for the task that appears in the syllabus. In a one-page, single-spaced, twelve-point font commentary, students must concisely explain what they learned that is important to them, tell why they find it important, and then describe how they will apply that learning to their personal and professional lives.

The best memos are both insightful and inspiring by clearly demonstrating self-awareness and self-reflection, by providing detailed examples of lessons learned, and by showing pertinent and timely ways students will apply those lessons. In other words, students indicate where their heads are at.

A powerful experiential exercise that demonstrates these steps is the flying device game. This is an activity based on an actual, life-and-death event. The famous scene in *Apollo 13* about "Square Peg in a Round Hole" inspired this game. The scene and the game address three skills: the ability to think critically to solve problems; the talent to assess an opportunity (even in difficult circumstances); and the requirement to leverage resources, even when there are not very many available.

In the game, teams of five to seven students must create a device that flies the farthest and the straightest. They can only use the materials that are assembled in the kit. Then someone on the team must launch the device in an open area somewhere outside the classroom.

Some things to note: Everything students need to know is in the instructions and in the kit. The instructions indicate that the teams have twenty-five minutes to complete the assignment, but the teacher changes that to fifteen minutes before they pick up their kits. The instructor specifically says "device" and not airplane. There are limited resources, which include things like a two-foot-by-three-foot poster board, paper plates, a sheet of aluminum foil, paper cups, paper clips, clothespins, scissors, scotch tape, tongue depressors, rubber bands . . . in other words, a wide range of possible building materials. Students are told there are prizes to the winning team!

Students have a great time with this experiential learning activity. They dash to get their kits, spread all the materials out, and set to work testing their devices. They are back in the classroom in exactly fifteen minutes; then they head outside to launch what they have created. That's when the surprises occur.

There is always a team or two that uses the poster board to fold into a paper airplane. That device always fails. Other teams come up with flying saucers, cups launched with rubber bands, and a variety of contraptions around which they have used up a full roll of scotch tape. The winning team usually does not build any of these. Instead, the winning team will roll up the aluminum foil with something heavy inside and heave it down the launching runway.

The debrief is enlightening as students address a range of questions such as "Isn't a flying device really an airplane?" "Is it fair to just heave a heavy ball?" "What is actually creative?" "Did all team members take time to listen to all proposed ideas?" "What is the role of competition [prizes awarded] in the creative process?" "What is required to communicate effectively when one has limited time and limited resources?"

During the discussion, students begin to focus on key learnings by relating the game to the dire situation in the scene from *Apollo 13*. Further lessons start to emerge such as beginning with the end in mind (farthest and straightest wins), as Stephen Covey recommends in *The*

Seven Habits of Highly Effective People, recognizing that there is an elegance to simplicity, being willing to listen to the ideas of all members of a team, discovering the value of trial and error in finding out what works and what doesn't. Through their follow-up experience memos, students often go further in internalizing their takeaways from this game. (See exhibit 9 in the appendix.)

THE APPLICATION

The real test of experiential learning comes when students apply their takeaways to other conditions and situations. They begin to take to heart the adage to "always know where your head is at." When students take from an experience something that is personal, emotional and useful to them, they more easily apply that learning to other situations.

There is an experiential exercise that initially mystifies students. The activity requires them to create the "worst business ever!" They must create a business (or other type of organization) that is doomed to fail, that cannot succeed under any circumstances, that is a disaster from start to finish. This activity is so counterintuitive that it stuns students, especially business school students. They have always been told to create a business that will succeed. They have never been asked to create a business to fail.

In teams of four to five, students proceed to come up with doomed enterprises. Some examples: selling meat in India, the Kim Kardashian Marriage Counseling Service, the do-it-yourself home surgery kit, paper nails, and so on. Students get wonderfully creative in devising businesses that cannot succeed. Then, the doomed business concept is given to another team, which is asked to transform the failed idea into a more viable venture. As a last step, the entire class participates in further revising the concepts to make it potentially successful. And the transformations occur.

Students sell meat in India to tourists at select hotels catering to foreigners, or they use plant-based burgers for Indians (not so impossible). The Kim Kardashian Marriage Counseling Service becomes a reality television show (people would actually watch that!). The do-it-yourself home surgery kit becomes a video game. The paper nails become part of a paper skyscraper construction package.

In the debrief, students begin to reassess the entire process of idea generation. They get a sense that perhaps there are no bad ideas but just different levels of viable ideas, some much less viable at the start than others.

They understand that ideas evolve, that they can take different shapes, and that a final idea may be quite different from an initial one. They experience the power of getting input from others about their ideas and the need to seek feedback. They recognize the importance of listening to the suggestions of others during ideation, no matter how crazy those thoughts might seem. They begin to sense how to shape a vision of what actually might be possible to do. Because this experience is personal, emotional, and useful, students apply the lessons to other endeavors in which they are involved. (See exhibit 10 in the appendix.)

A range of experiential learning opportunities can apply to any discipline: elevator pitches to present one's ideas, business plan competitions and idea competitions, interviews with outside experienced individuals, expert presenters as speakers in one's classes, company tours, simulations that emulate various situations, case studies in which students role-play participants in the case or in which the protagonist themselves discuss the actual situation after students critique the situation.

FLIPPING THE CLASSROOM

Experiential learning can also take other forms. Teachers can flip their classrooms.

Flipping the classroom shifts instruction to a learner-centered versus teacher-centered model. To increase student engagement and learning, students listen to online lectures and complete readings at home while actively working on hands-on activities in the classroom. In other words, teachers reverse the traditional approach to learning. They deliver foundation content in a discipline often through short video lectures of eight to twelve minutes and through selected readings that students complete at home, and then they follow that up in the classroom with more direct experiential learning activities.

In more quantitative disciplines like finance, economics, statistics, and accounting and in disciplines in the sciences, teachers create an active learning environment in which students learn at their own pace and teachers focus more time to work with each student individually. In the flipped classroom, the role of the teacher changes. It becomes more personalized and less didactic. The teacher acts more as a mentor or guide rather than a traditional lecturer downloading information. This is a demanding role for the teacher, who must observe students closely, provide immediate feedback, assess student work as it is happening, and guide students in their learning experience.

The teacher provides foundational information on the course topic via assigned readings, sets up lecture and demonstration videos that they prepare or are prepared by a third party, and arranges online class discussions for students to complete at home.

In the classroom, teachers redefine in-class activities. They implement active learning strategies. These include hands-on problem solving and lab experiments, original document analysis, project-based assignments, debates, formal presentations, and even current event discussions on issues related to the course topic. They thus use classroom time to explore topics in more depth and to create more meaningful learning opportunities for their students.

In the flipped classroom, the key elements of experiential learning are still present. The teacher must clearly identify and define the purpose of each classroom activity, shape an exercise that addresses that purpose, help their students debrief their learning experience, and then assist students in applying their own learning. When this happens, the flipped classroom can provide engaging and impactful experiential learning.

Experiential learning is a powerful teaching technique. It creates a really different learning environment for students . . . and for the teacher. Because it focuses on the key goals of the course and specific objectives of a class, requires hands-on involvement, encourages a positive attitude, and emphasizes reflection and application, experiential learning enlivens the classroom by surprising and engaging students. Most important, experiential learning sets a foundation for lifelong learning.

If students begin to understand how to learn from experiences that they encounter in the classroom, then perhaps they also learn how to apply lesson from any experience that they may encounter during their lives. If that happens, they will always know where their heads are at.

Section III

Teaching for Excitement

Takeaways

Section III has provided perspectives on "Teaching for Excitement." It points out how to design and deliver an engaging and interactive lecture by following a know-feel-do approach to a topic. It suggests implementing a range of techniques, such as viewing a lecture as an event, labeling the speaking experience positively, utilizing redundancy, and including short writes to make a teacher's lecture personal, insightful, and memorable.

To add a been-there, done-that dimension to a class, the section shows how to identify, prepare, and direct outside guest speakers to ensure that they make a substantive and stimulating contribution to a teacher's course.

Then, by incorporating experiential techniques and activities, such as the bag resume, jazz session, and flying device game, teachers can include hands-on learning experiences to enliven their classrooms.

Think about three takeaways related to how you build excitement in your own calling. Consider: What is your approach to presenting and communicating with others? How do you use the experience of others in your courses? What kind of teacher has experience been for you?

Specific takeaways might include utilizing the know-feel-do strategy for your next lecture, consciously owning your classroom the next time you walk into it, having coffee or lunch with a potential guest speaker to learn their story and determine whether it can contribute to the goals of your class, and creating your own bag resume to consider what items to use and why you selected them.

SECTION IV

Beyond the Classroom

Chapter 10

What Makes Yoda So Good?

Over the years, teachers have had countless meetings with students. Some of these meetings are easily dismissed. They are the sessions in which students have begged, bribed, blamed, and threatened teachers to change a grade.

Some students will contend at the end of a semester that they really did better than their poor performance actually indicated, plead with their teacher about needing a higher grade, and beseech the teacher to raise their grade. Instead, students come to understand the importance of consequences.

Some students will try to make a teacher an offer they can't refuse. They may suggest that cash or a bottle of wine or some other type of compensation could be provided if only the teacher upped their grade a bit. Instead, students learn that some offers can be refused.

Students who fail a course may castigate a teacher for not making sure that they attended class and completed their assignments. Therefore, since the student's failure is the fault of the teacher, the teacher should give the student a passing grade. Instead, students get a lesson on personal responsibility.

There are also the students who warn a teacher that their parent is a trustee and could cause the teacher some difficulty if the teacher is not more flexible in reassessing their grade. Still, the grade stays the same.

Then there are the meetings with students that really are important. Students seek out teachers for advice about which major to choose, which job offer to take, and ways to deal with a crisis in their lives. A student may tell a teacher that they have been diagnosed with cancer, are undergoing chemotherapy, and are wondering how to stay in the class. In discussion with another student, a teacher may notice the signs of depression and indications of suicidal thoughts, and must find a way to put the student in contact with professional help.

In other words, while some meetings with students are frivolous or simply distractions, others involve profound, even life-affecting decisions that students are facing such as which career choice to make, how to deal with a family conflict, and what to do in the midst of a personal or medical crisis.

In these meetings, students are placing trust in their teacher. They are seeking guidance to sort out the options they face. They are asking the teacher to be not just a sounding board for their concerns but also an advisor to assist them in determining their course of action.

In these defining situations, a teacher cannot make a decision for a student. But a teacher can help them understand their options, consider the pros and cons of the condition in which they find themselves, and assist them in evaluating various courses of action. In other words, a teacher can act as a guide for them as they choose the direction in which to go.

"Guide" is a good metaphor for the role that teachers are sometimes asked to play beyond the classroom. It reflects a key responsibility for a teacher—to serve as a mentor to the students under their tutelage. A teacher cannot dictate which path a student should take or which course of action they should follow. But a teacher can assist them in understanding what may lie ahead, provide insight on the terrain that they may have to traverse, help prepare them for their journey, and support them in the decisions that they make. In other words, teachers can serve as mentors to their students.

Mentors can have a profound impact on a person's personal and professional lives. They can help a person on their journey to take advantage of opportunity, to deal with adversity, and to more clearly understand their strengths and weaknesses.

The original Mentor was a character who appeared in Homer's *Odyssey* as the trusted friend of Odysseus, who asked him to look after his son, Telemakhos. Thereafter, time and again in literature, the mentor—like Merlin to Arthur and Charlotte to Wilbur—appeared at the outset of a person's journey as a guide, equipping their charge to deal with whatever might come. The modern cultural version of the ideal mentor, Yoda to Luke, has become a model for how to influence, support, and develop a promising mentee.

In the second Star Wars film, *The Empire Strikes Back*, Luke Skywalker discovers that he needs help on his journey to become a Jedi Knight. He finds what initially seems to be an unlikely guide for such a momentous journey. He meets Yoda on an isolated planet in the galaxy. The elfish character puts up with Luke's initial insolence and arrogance, takes him under his pointed ears, and manages to bring out the Knight that is within him. But what is it that makes Yoda so good as a mentor? What is it about Yoda's mentoring attributes that can actually help reinvigorate and renew a teacher's commitment to their own mighty purpose?[1]

Mentors like Yoda support their mentees. They commit time to the relationship and show empathy for another's concerns, hopes, and aspirations. They listen actively to focus full attention when someone brings them problems or seeks their advice. They build trust by serving as an advocate for another and by continually encouraging a mentee's efforts. They help their charge to reflect on their experiences. In other words, they have their backs.

Mentors like Yoda offer challenges to create an environment for another to learn. They assign tasks to take on new roles and wider responsibilities. They engage in discussions to provide candid and constructive feedback to help a mentee better assess their strengths and weaknesses. They debrief teachable moments with them that provide new insights on how to solve problems, take advantage of opportunities, and hone one's skills.

Importantly, they provide a vision that helps another person catch a glimpse of their own potential and their future possible self. They serve as a model that the journey can be made and that provides a mirror on what one might be able to accomplish. In other words, they help a mentee look ahead and chart their course in life. In the process, the mentee gains confidence in their own abilities and eventually achieves independence, even from their mentor.

Real mentoring is difficult. It is more than advising, coaching, or giving directions. There are pitfalls that can kill a mentoring relationship, but ones that teachers who are effective as mentors know how to avoid:

- *Don't allocate time.* Instead, effective teachers-as-mentors always seem to allocate time to their students, set high standards, and express positive expectations. They facilitate intentional learning by creating opportunities for one to develop their skills and by exposing them to different experiences.

- *Lecture a lot.* Instead, the successful mentor talks less and listens more. They are anxious to hear a student's thoughts, ask probing questions, and consider the student's recommendations.
- *Tell war stories.* A good teacher-mentor never harps. They do not need to try to impress a student with important things that they have done.
- *Criticize everything.* Rather than tear a student down, a confident mentor constantly seeks to build them up with honest dialogue. They respect and even celebrate another's accomplishments.
- *Breach confidentiality.* Instead, the teaching Yoda maintains confidences. They never talk behind a student's back, and they keep the promises they make. They enjoy watching a student develop and grow. They genuinely like sharing their knowledge and experience.

For a teacher, the opportunity to serve as a mentor is a gift from their students. Their willingness to seek their teacher's advice, their trust in their teacher having their best interests at heart, and their openness to confide their issues and concerns to their teacher are among the most rewarding privileges of teaching. Consequently, teachers must try to be a Yoda to their students—to support those who come under their tutelage, create challenges and opportunities that allow their students to learn and to flourish, listen with care and understanding, and provide a vision for them of what their future selves could be.

There is something noble about the character of a person who takes the time, care, energy, and commitment to serve as a mentor for another. Maybe this is what makes Yoda so good. He demonstrates nobility of character in making a difference in Luke's life. Teachers who take on the role and responsibility of mentoring demonstrate their own nobility of character in making a difference in the lives of their students. In the process, they not only hone their craft but also bring luster to their profession.

Chapter 11

Epilogue

Purveyors of Hope

As a teacher pursues their own mighty purpose in their discipline, they should recognize a fundamental truth about teaching and learning. People learn what they want to learn. It's that simple. If one does not want to learn something, then they won't. Whether that person is an elementary or high school student, an undergraduate in college, or an executive in a leadership development program, they will learn only what they want to learn.

Consequently, it is up to the teacher to do everything they can to make their students want to learn what they are teaching. To do that, a teacher needs to inspire and not just inform. That inspiration has to start with the teacher themselves.

SEEKING INSPIRATION

Teachers who inspire their students need to feel inspired themselves. So, they look for inspiration. They seek it out. Fortunately for them, inspiration can come from near and far.

A teacher can find inspiration in their own family. They can be dazzled by the accomplishments of their spouse, the talents of their sons and daughters, and the calm joy of sharing family events.

Friends and colleagues in one's own discipline can motivate a teacher by sharing their knowledge, wisdom, and passion for teaching. Their camaraderie through conferences and professional development programs can fire up a teacher all over again to do well in the classroom.

A teacher can take immense encouragement from the collaboration that they have in developing new programs with colleagues and learning from the experiences of others.

A teacher can value and take encouragement from the feedback they receive from students as part of a course evaluation. They can follow the suggestions for improvement that students offer. In addition, teachers can celebrate their students' accomplishments inside and outside the classroom. They can enjoy knowing that they are contributing to the development and success of others, especially when former students reach back to thank them for making a difference in their lives.

A teacher can treasure the unique perspective of those from outside their discipline who provide points of view that are different from their own and who share insights to improve their performance in the classroom.

A teacher can take heart in the compelling stories of role models in their discipline. They can celebrate those who innovate, overcome adversity, demonstrate innovation and creativity, enhance community well-being, and act ethically and morally.

A teacher can look for inspirational books, writings, and quotes that spark fresh ways for them to think and act. They can incorporate those in their classes and in their interactions with their students.

Every teacher in every discipline leads students on a journey of self-discovery. On that journey, a teacher focuses on helping students recognize, assess, and pursue opportunity; capitalize on their creative and innovative talents; practice "yes, and" behavior; make the most of limited resources; and create not only value but also meaning for themselves and for those with whom they interact.

An inspired teacher points direction but never dictates it. Warns of hazards but never prevents them. Doesn't predict but does challenge. Debriefs success and acknowledges the power of failure. Recognizes talent but rewards hard work. Encourages hope and bets on potential.

Inspired teachers always perform at their best in each class. Performance combines substance (real content) and form (genuine interest). Both are essential. If a teacher is not deeply engaged and personally enthused with what they are teaching, and visibly show these by their performance, then why would their students be? By performing at their best, teachers can inspire and not just tally grades.

STAY CURIOUS

An old adage is that curiosity killed the cat. No, it didn't. It gave it nine lives! To be inspired is to stay curious, to find new things to think about and do, to consider novel methods and approaches, to view ways to create and implement through a different lens.

In his wonderful biography of Leonardo da Vinci, Walter Isaacson emphasizes Leonardo's unquenchable curiosity.[1] Perhaps no other human being has been as curious about all things great and small as Leonardo. Whether it was human and animal anatomy, architecture, fanciful mechanics like flying machines, optics, painting of course, or even the tongue of a woodpecker, Leonardo wanted to learn about it, design it, draw it, apply it, and improve upon it.

After considering Leonardo's remarkable range of interests and accomplishments, one may not be able to be as curious as he was, but a teacher can aspire to be as curious as they possibly can. In turn, they can encourage their students to be curious as well. To stay curious, a teacher can work at developing their "to-learn" list (somewhat like Leonardo developed in his daily journal of things to investigate). They can ask their students to take responsibility for their own learning by developing their to-learn list at the start of each class.

A teacher can be glad to be distracted by an activity entirely different from their discipline, like a compelling avocation such as fly-fishing, simply because it is a wonderful way to experience something completely novel. A curious teacher can reach out to seek feedback on what they write, how they teach, and what they can do to improve. They can collaborate with others who have different perspectives, expertise, and experience from themselves. They can consciously reflect on what works and what does not in their classrooms.

THE BEST VIRTUE

Hope is the abiding virtue of teachers. The best teachers are purveyors of hope. With hope, all things are possible. With hope comes the belief that one can make good things happen, that a person can have a positive influence over their condition, that one can grow and improve.

There is a story of an entrepreneur who had failed at several previous ventures, losing the money of the investor who had funded each previous effort. The entrepreneur had an idea for yet another new enterprise. Going back to that same investor who had lost money on every other venture, the entrepreneur asked the investor to fund yet another opportunity. The investor, in trying to be kind, told the entrepreneur, "You have a number of blemishes in your past." To which, the entrepreneur replied, "That may be true, but my future is spotless!"

A teacher's future is spotless. So is the future of each and every student in their classes. To have the privilege of contributing to that future, to influence it in a constructive way, to have the chance to make a positive difference in the future of another is a remarkable gift. By utilizing the tools and artistry of the craft of teaching, a teacher can kindle an ardent desire to learn. For a teacher, there is joy in that.

Section IV

Beyond the Classroom
Takeaways

Section IV has looked "Beyond the Classroom." It emphasizes the ongoing role of teachers as mentors to their students. It highlights the metaphor of teacher-as-guide for their students who are on a journey of self-discovery. It provides guidelines for effective mentorship, such as allocating time, active listening, maintaining confidences, and celebrating a mentee's accomplishments.

This section reminds teachers to seek inspiration for themselves through their family, their colleagues, their students, and their own approach to their craft of teaching. It encourages teachers to be curious by developing their own to-earn list, finding a compelling avocation, and discovering new ways to collaborate with others.

Think about three takeaways related to your own next steps. Consider: Who has mentored you, and how have you mentored others? What do you do to stay inspired and be curious? What changes will you make in your own teaching?

Specific takeaways might include contacting someone who has been a mentor to you and explaining how they have made a difference in your life; evaluating a genuinely important meeting with a student to assess how well you may have served as a mentor; developing your own to-learn list; considering a hobby or avocation that you have wanted to start and then starting it; and identifying one teaching skill, technique, or approach that you want to improve and then indicating how you will go about improving it.

Further Reading

Ahearn, David, Frank Ford, and David Wilk. *Happy Accidents: The Transformative Power of "Yes, And" at Work and in Life.* Hoboken, NJ: Wiley, 2017.

Daly, John A. *Advocacy: Championing Ideas and Influencing Others.* New Haven, CT: Yale University Press, 2012.

Darden, Mary Landon. *Entrepreneuring the Future of Higher Education: Radical Transformation in Times of Profound Change.* Lanham, MD: Rowman & Littlefield, 2021.

Heath, Chip, and Dan Heath. *Made to Stick: Why Some Ideas Survive and Others Die.* New York: Random House, 2008.

Kawasaki, Guy. *The Art of the Start 2.0: The Time-Tested, Battle-Hardened Guide for Anyone Starting Anything.* New York: Portfolio/Penguin, 2015.

Leonard, Kelly, and Tom Yorton. *Yes, And: How Improvisation Reverses "No, But" Thinking and Improves Creativity and Collaboration.* New York: HarperCollins, 2015.

Mycoskie, Blake. *Start Something That Matters.* New York: Spiegel & Grau, 2011.

Robinson, Sir Ken, and Lou Aronica. *Creative Schools: The Grassroots Revolution That's Transforming Education.* New York: Penguin, 2016.

Sawyer, Keith. *The Creative Classroom: Innovative Teaching for 21st Century Learners.* New York: Teachers College Press, 2019.

Smilor, Ray. *Daring Visionaries: How Entrepreneurs Build Companies, Inspire Allegiance and Create Wealth.* Avon, MA: Adams Media, 2001.

Acknowledgments

This book started long before I actually began to write it.

As I look back, I realize the profound influence that former teachers of mine have had on me. Some of these teachers have passed on. I recall them with affection and gratitude: Carrie Abbott, George Kozmetsky, Michie Slaughter, Brother Simon Scribner, H. Wayne Morgan, Brother Hilarion Brezik, Claude Nolan, Brother Stephen Walsh, Jeffry Timmons, and Rob Rhodes.

Each year for the past twenty-two years, I have taught in the Experiential Classroom. My colleagues in this teacher training program have inspired me every year with their passion, creativity, and commitment to teaching excellence: Don Kuratko, Rebecca White, Jeff Stamp, Ernie Cadotte, Debbie Brock, Alex De Noble, Karl Vespar, Dave Rosenthal, Leyland Pitt, Minet Schindehutte, Greg Fisher, John Mullins, Dave Newton, Alex Bruton, Jerry Katz, Jamie Kraft, John Dobson, and Frank Moyes.

At Texas Christian University, colleagues have inspired me with their commitment to teaching: Suzanne Carter, Brad Hancock, Eric Simanek, Phil Hartman, and Michael Kruger.

I am grateful to Frank Hernandez, founding member of Deans for Impact and the dean of the College of Education at TCU, for writing the foreword for this book.

I have benefited from the thoughtful input of Norval Kneten, Susan McDonald, Georgy Laptev, and Sunil Shukla.

I feel a special sense of gratitude to others who have read multiple versions of this book as it was being written and provided insightful, challenging, and caring suggestions along the way to improve it. Dan

Short made valuable comments on the book by combining a sharp wit with persistence in making his points. Michael Morris provided thoughtful and creative feedback. Magnus Rittby provided invaluable insights and important clarifications. Tahita Fulkerson shared her knowledge of teaching and made helpful recommendations. Jana Matthews brought her usual sharp eye and incisive comments to reviewing the manuscript.

I have received candid and gracious feedback, insights, and recommendations from many friends and colleagues as I have been working on this book. Many of these suggestions I have implemented. In all cases, I have taken each and every one to heart. Any shortcomings in this book are only and entirely my own.

Tom Koerner, vice president and senior executive editor of the Education Division at Rowman & Littlefield, made invaluable recommendations on the manuscript and steered its publication with enthusiasm and professionalism. Thank you, Tom. I have appreciated the support of Kira Hall, assistant editor for education at R&L.

I have been fortunate to enjoy the unqualified affection, unfailing goodwill, and completely biased support of my family. My brother, John, read versions of the book and offered his suggestions. More than that, he provided continuous encouragement. I have appreciated the thoughtfulness of my daughter-in-law, Melissa, and the good spirit of Julie Reichenberger.

My sons inspire me constantly. I am dazzled by the dedication, entrepreneurial talent, and project management abilities of my son, Matthew, who is also a gifted teacher. This book would not have been possible without him. He provided meaningful insights and recommendations, was essential in assembling the manuscript over several revisions, and did it all with great good spirit. I am awed by the preparation, discipline, and commitment of my son, Kevin, and impressed by the calm joy that he displays after a hard ultra race well run.

My two granddaughters, Natalie (10) and Samantha (4.5), provided endless joy during the writing of this book. I could always count on them to be willing to play with me, remind me not to take myself too seriously, and show me the happiness of just being silly.

My greatest thanks is to my wonderful and beautiful wife, Judy. I am grateful for her constant support, love, and encouragement.

How did I get so lucky!

Appendix: Exhibits 1–10

EXHIBIT 1: HALF OF THIRTEEN EXERCISE

Purpose: To encourage a willingness to be wrong.

Exercise: To generate as many ways as possible to consider what is half of the number thirteen.

- The teacher asks, "What is half of thirteen?"
- The teacher affirms each and every answer with a positive response.
- The teacher continues to ask, "What else is half of thirteen?"
- The teacher is nonjudgmental, avoids criticizing any answer, and lists every answer on the board.

Activity: During the discussion, students offer a range of possibilities.

- The initial student responses are almost always six and a half, or 6.5, or some other numerical form, such as thirteen divided by two.
- The teacher congratulates each response.
- A student will eventually begin to consider other options, such as one and three, which then others may divide horizontally and diagonally. The teacher rewards the responses with positive comments.
- Once the floodgates open, students venture other answers, such as "thir" and "teen," which suggests other languages. A student may offer "e," which is the middle (half) letter in Spanish of thirteen, *trece*.

- Other responses may be 06:30 (which refers to military time) and half a baker's dozen (which ties in donuts). A student or the teacher may suggest alternatives, such as a consideration of roman numerals, XIII, which then allows for answers such as eleven, two, six, and eight.

Lessons for discussion:

- When confronting a problem or opportunity, the first response is often the most obvious and familiar, which is usually taught as correct, and the least creative.
- There is never just one answer or alternative available. There are always different ways to look at a situation.
- Persistence is key to solving problems and taking advantage of opportunities.
- The role of the teacher (or leader) is critical. What happens if the teacher tells the student who suggests one and three that their answer is stupid and wrong? Then all possible responses cease, students become fearful of offering a suggestion, and creativity comes to a halt.
- Creativity requires a willingness to be wrong, to offer the unconventional suggestion, to propose the idea from left field. That takes some internal fortitude.

EXHIBIT 2: ROUND OBJECTS EXERCISE

Purpose: To demonstrate conceptual blending as a source of creativity.
Exercise: Students make a list of round objects in ninety seconds.
Activity: The teacher directs an interactive exercise.

- The teacher gives students one directive: make a list of round objects, which they write down on a sheet of paper.
- During the ninety seconds that students are given to do the assignment, the teacher calls out the time: "Sixty seconds left," "Forty-five seconds left," and so on to "Fifteen seconds left," and then "Stop."
- The teacher leads a debrief of the lists by asking what things students listed first. The usual answer is some kind of ball, which is what seems most common and obvious when thinking of a round object and is the least creative. Students will then begin to make other connections: planets, coins, and fruit. Then, they start to make more ingenious connections to body parts, food, construction materials, weather patterns, and so on. Their minds make unconventional relationships to the concept of roundness.
- The teacher will then ask who has an item that no one else in the class has listed. A range of innovative connections emerge: manhole cover, rings of Saturn, wheels of various kinds, and so on.
- As a last step, the teacher asks students to simply count the number of items that they have listed and then asks, "Who has five or more?" All hands go up. Then ten or more, fifteen or more, twenty or more. There are usually one or two students who will have listed more than twenty items.

Lessons for discussion:

- When confronted with a problem or issue, one will usually start with the most obvious and least creative—a ball of some kind.
- Quantity leads to quality. The more items one can generate, the greater the chance of something really significant emerging.
- Originality has to do with novelty—the item that no one else has listed.

- Focusing on a clear objective—like a list of round objects—clarifies the goal and gets everyone contributing to finding the best alternative.
- Drive—continually pushing to list as many items as possible—is essential to finding creative alternatives and important to have in any team effort.

EXHIBIT 3: DOTS EXERCISE

Purpose: To demonstrate the power of trial and error in the creative process.

Exercise: Students are asked to connect all nine dots with one line without lifting their pencils from the paper.

Activity: The teacher passes out a paper with nine dots in a tic-tac-toe arrangement. The directive on the paper tells students to make a line through all nine dots without lifting their pencils from the paper.

- Students individually or with others try to complete the challenge.
- When a student has a solution, the teacher calls the student to the board and has them show the answer to the rest of the class.
- Then, the teacher tells the students to solve the problem with three lines. And again has the student who solves the problem come up and show the rest of the class.
- The teacher then tells the students to solve the problem not with two lines but with only one.

Lessons for discussion:

- Everyone makes mistakes (i.e., we fail), but we learn.
- We don't call the learning failure but rather gaining knowledge through trial and error, which is essential to creativity.
- The more limited the resources (from four lines to one), the more creative we are forced to be.
- Solutions to problems occur when we alter the conditions in which we find ourselves. With only one line, students may suggest a paintbrush instead of a pencil, or cut up or fold the paper to align the dots, or roll up the paper and use a circular line.

EXHIBIT 4: PRECOURSE INVITATION TO CLASS

Welcome to the course!

It's great to have you in this class. I'm excited to have the opportunity to teach—and to be taught by—each one of you. I promise that I will bring my best thinking, highest energy, and greatest enthusiasm to our class . . . and will ask you to do the same.

We will hit the ground running! From the first moment, I will ask you to think outside the proverbial box, tap your own creative and innovative talents, and participate actively in the course. You can expect the unexpected, anticipate ambiguous circumstances, and plan to get outside of your comfort zone—in other words, a fun and productive learning experience!

You should read the syllabus here (or online) to see the coming attractions, which are full of action and adventure. Experiential exercises so that we learn by doing, interactive lectures that will call on your experience and know-how as we learn from each other, and cases/activities/competitions to hone your problem-solving skills.

I have found Mark Twain's observation to be true: "Twenty years from now you will be more disappointed by the things that you didn't do than by the ones that you did do. So, throw off the bowlines. Sail away from the safe harbor. Catch the trade winds in your sails. Explore. Dream. Discover." Just as you are doing in pursuing your degree.

Or as that great America philosopher of the twentieth century, Yogi Berra, advised: "When you come to a fork in the road, take it!" At any rate, we'll take a couple of forks in the road during the class . . . games and prizes included!

Some things to look forward to and get ready for:

- [Highlight unique techniques, models, and tools that the class will utilize.]
- [Identify one major individual or team activity that students will experience and explain why it will be fun.]
- [Describe one or two experiential exercises to make learning unconventional and exciting.]
- [Explain why one of the books in the course is a favorite of yours and why they will find it enjoyable to read.]

But wait, there's more!

- [Tell students about one totally unexpected learning opportunity that lies ahead.]
- [Promise students that they will have opportunities to apply their learning to their own situations through debriefs in class, writing experience memos, or consciously reflecting on their own learning.]
- [Require students to prepare a to-learn list—three things that they would like to learn in this class—and indicate that you will discuss these on the first day of class. You might even indicate your three.]
- [Remind them to come intending to learn, share, and have fun . . . and that you will too.]

I know what you must be thinking. . . . Can all this and even more be jam packed into one eventful course? Amazing but true!

If you have any questions or just would like to have a conversation, feel free to email, call, or set up a visit. Let's get started!

EXHIBIT 5: FORCED PAIRS EXERCISE

Purpose: To demonstrate the "yes, and" philosophy.

Exercise: To make unusual connections by matching what students love to do.

- The teacher asks students to list three things that they love to do.
- The teacher then tells students to meet with a partner and match their first items, second items, and third items.
- Students must then come up with a product or service that addresses the new connections.

Activity: During the exercise, students say, "Yes" to the match and then add, "And" by creating possibilities from the match.

- Students may identify a range of things that they love to do, such as travel, knit, fish, golf, read, even eat and sleep.
- By then matching their activities, they demonstrate bisociation, which is the ability to connect the unconnectable and relate the unrelatable.
- Students learn to discover possibilities by avoiding "no, but" and inventing ways to connect their items.
- Students affirm their partner's suggestion and then add something new and positive to the match.

Lessons for discussion:

- Students have great fun with this exercise and are enthusiastic to discuss their matches.
- They learn to be open to possibilities, even when the connections are wildly different and apparently initially impossible to match.
- The exercise demonstrates the importance of accepting ideas from others and working with others to shape and modify ideas.
- Discussion can then focus on how students should respond to the ideas of teammates in projects, how collaboration can be improved by being receptive to the ideas of others, and how "yes, and" can enhance the creative process.

(This exercise was adapted from a session on experiential learning at an annual conference of the United States Association of Small Business and Entrepreneurship.)

EXHIBIT 6: MEMORANDUM TO
OUTSIDE SPEAKERS

To: Panel of three speakers to address class
From: The teacher
Re: Title of class

Date and location of class

It has been a pleasure for me to meet with each of you to learn about your experience and to discuss how you can make a terrific contribution to the students in my class. By focusing on the challenges and strategies for running a successful organization with vivid examples of what you have done and by highlighting what you have learned, you can create a wonderful learning experience for each student. I know that we will have a lively, provocative, and interesting session.

I would like to use this memo to set the stage for your presentation to and interaction with the students. I'll pose the types of questions that I will ask so that you can start to consider your responses. In addition, I'll offer some suggestions to help make our interaction during the panel discussion as enjoyable and successful as possible. Then, I'll explain my role in this process.

Questions

The purpose of these questions is to spur thought, be a bit unconventional, and get the students really interested in what you have to say. So, you can expect me to pose the following types of questions:

- What is the most important thing that you do in your organization that makes a real difference in its success? How do you know?
- What is the smartest thing that you ever done in developing your organization? Why was it so smart?
- What has been your darkest day? What made it so difficult?
- If you could do something differently, what would that be?
- How do you communicate the vision and values of your organization? What techniques, approaches, and methods have you utilized?
- If you could give one or two pieces of advice to other leaders, what would you tell them?

Suggestions

Tell stories. This is the surest way to be effective in this type of format. Students love to hear someone give an example, recount an incident, or describe an episode that demonstrates an important point. Rather than say that your organization is dedicated to making positive changes, for example, tell a story about what you did or what one of your employees did that proves the point. Stories and examples are insightful, engaging, and entertaining—a great combination.

Personalize your response. Students want to know what *you* think, how *you* feel, and what *you* did. For example, if a student asks you about how you started your organization, talk about what you personally went through to get going.

Be concise. Long-winded answers lose students, and they are not fair to the other panelists. In addition to our discussion, we would like to get in as many questions from the students as possible. So, please be focused in your responses.

View as a conversation. We will be seated in comfortable chairs in a semicircle in the front of the class. Think of this as a lively conversation among friends. Feel free to jump in with a comment, add to what another is saying, or give a different point of view, just as you would in a conversation. I'll manage the dialogue process.

My Role

My role is to pose initial questions and then follow up with additional questions to bring out your insights. It's also up to me to keep the discussion moving and to make sure everyone has a chance to participate. Please understand if I curtail your response to move on to another topic or to let someone else provide their perspective.

Thank you for bringing your knowledge, experience, and wisdom to this class session. I know the students are looking forward to it as am I. It's great to have you in the course!

If you have any questions, please give me a call.

EXHIBIT 7: THE BAG RESUME EXERCISE

Purpose: To build an esprit de corps in the class.

Exercise: To have each student introduce themselves in an unconventional way.

- Each student is given a brown paper grocery bag.
- They then must introduce themselves by pulling six items out of their bag that explain the main influences in their lives.
- Students have two minutes to describe how each item has contributed to who they are.

Activity: During the exercise, students demonstrate creativity, take a risk, and provide insights into what shaped them.

- The role of the teacher is critical because the teacher sets the example for the exercise on the first day of class by pulling items from their own bag resume.
- A resume is usually thought of as a piece of paper that describes one's experience, education, and skills. The bag resume focuses instead on the people, activities, and events that actually shape one's personality.
- Items in the bag may include things like photographs, sports equipment, bibles, heirlooms, keepsakes and mementos from loved ones, symbols of a challenge in one's life, or an adversity confronted.

Lessons for discussion:

- By connecting a grocery bag with a resume, the exercise demonstrates bisociation, which is part of the creative process.
- Presenting the items requires some risk taking since many students will reveal something personal and meaningful for them.
- The exercise helps students gain an understanding of the uniqueness of their peers, builds relationships within the class, and encourages respect and inclusiveness.
- Students become engaged in a debrief of the exercise by discussing how and why they chose their items, what they learned about others in the class, and how the experience might influence how they interact with others.

EXHIBIT 8: THE JAZZ SESSION EXERCISE

Purpose: To demonstrate improvisation.
Exercise: Students must create an original musical composition in fifteen minutes using readily available instruments.

- The teacher puts students in teams of six to nine.
- Each group selects a leader to conduct the development of the composition.
- Everyone in the team is responsible for creating and performing a unique composition. That is, students cannot do a variation of "Happy Birthday" or "The Star-Spangled Banner."
- Each member of the group must play a musical instrument. The teacher can provide some instruments of they wish, such as drums, triangles, whistles, bells, and so forth. Students can also utilize their own instruments such as tabletops, books, snapping their fingers, bottles, and even their own voices.
- Teams have fifteen minutes to develop and rehearse their composition.
- Each team must then perform the composition for two full minutes with the teacher timing it. The team cannot stop before the full two minutes is completed.

Lessons for discussion:

- Students are surprised by this because many will claim they are not musicians. But they must perform anyway.
- The results are often amazing.
- Teams do indeed create and perform an original composition and have fun doing it.
- During the performance, some students will shed their inhibitions by dancing, singing, and even engaging the audience of their fellow students to enhance the performance.
- The two-minute performance requirement is important. Often students will need to improvise within the improvisation to keep the composition going for the full time.
- The debrief opens a wide range of topics for discussion: What did students learn about improvisation? How did they communicate

within their team? What was it like to perform? What happened when a team member took the lead to improvise within the improvisation? How does the behavior of one person influence the behavior of others on a team? How can they apply improvisation to other aspects of their work and life?

(This exercise was designed by Minet Schindehutte, who teaches at Syracuse University.)

EXHIBIT 9: THE FLYING DEVICE GAME

Purpose: To demonstrate problem-solving skills and the ability to leverage limited resources.

Exercise: To build and fly a device that goes the farthest and straightest.

- Students are put in teams of five to seven members.
- The teacher assembles kits with a wide range of potential building materials, such as poster board, paper plates and cups, aluminum foil, tongue depressors, paper clips, a pair of scissors, a pen, and so forth. The same materials are in each kit.
- Students have fifteen minutes to build their device, after which they must have one member launch the device.
- The winning team has the device that goes the farthest and straightest. Everyone on the winning team gets a prize. The teacher is the official judge of the competition.

Activity: During the game, students work in teams to design a variety of devices.

- The game is based on a real-life situation from the movie *Apollo 13*, in which engineers must jury-rig a device to avoid carbon dioxide poisoning of the astronauts. The teacher shows the YouTube video clip.
- The teacher tells the students that everything they need to know is in the instructions and will thus answer no questions.
- The instructions indicate a "device," not an airplane, and indicate that the teams have twenty-five minutes for the activity (but the teacher changes that to fifteen minutes just before the teams pick up their kits).
- Once teams return to the classroom with their device, the entire class goes outside where a member of the team launches their device.

Lessons for discussion:

- There is always a team or two that makes an airplane from the poster board. This fails on launch. Other teams build a range of other devices.

- The design that usually wins is simply some kind of ball with weight that goes far and straight.
- The debrief can address a range of issues: What does this activity indicate about solving problems? What is creative about the exercise? How did teams utilize trial and error? Why did some make an airplane (most obvious and least creative)? How did the time change affect the view of the activity (added pressure)? Did teams start with the end in mind or simply rush to make various devices? Why is there an elegance to simplicity (as Stephen Covey emphasized)?
- After the debrief, the teacher gives a prize (like a 100 Grand candy bar) to each winning team member amid a round of applause.

EXHIBIT 10: THE WORST BUSINESS EVER!

Purpose: To demonstrate the idea generation process.
Exercise: Students must create a business (or other organization) that is doomed to fail.

- This counterintuitive activity surprises students because they have never been asked to create a business that cannot succeed.
- The teacher puts students in teams of four to five and tells them that they have five minutes to come up with a business that is a disaster and that cannot succeed under any circumstances.

Activity: In three steps during the exercise, students transform a failed idea into a potentially viable one.

- Step 1: In five minutes, student teams come up with a concept for a failed business (or other organization). The only criterion is that the business must be legal (they can't sell cocaine to kids). They have great fun in generating doomed concepts and in listening to the doomed concepts of other teams. The teacher writes each doomed business on the board.
- Step 2: The teacher assigns the doomed business to another team and gives that team ten minutes to revise the concept into something that could be potentially viable. The teacher writes the revised concepts on the board next to the doomed ideas.
- Step 3: The teacher opens the discussion of the revised concepts to the entire class for further revisions into potentially viable businesses and writes those suggestions on the board.

Lessons for discussion:

- Students learn to focus on the idea generation process by realizing that there are different levels of ideas, some more viable than others at the start. Some students may even point out that there are no bad ideas, just qualitative differences in ideas.
- Students begin to appreciate the importance of getting input from others, especially those with different knowledge, experience, and connections from their own.

- They recognize that there are benefits to listening to the suggestions of others during the brainstorming process no matter how crazy some suggestions might seem initially.
- Students also realize that opportunity may lie in unexpected places.

Notes

PREFACE

1. George Bernard Shaw, from *Man and Superman*, 1903, in the Epistle Dedicatory to Arthur Bingham Walkley, *Collected Plays with Their Prefaces*, vol. 2, ed. Dan H. Lawrence (London: Bodley Head Bernard Shaw, 1971).

2. Harvey Penick with Bud Shrake, *And If You Play Golf, You're My Friend: Further Reflections of a Grown Caddie* (New York: Simon & Schuster, 1993), 31.

INTRODUCTION

1. The quote about education, bottles or pails, and fire has generated a good deal of discussion about its accuracy and attribution. The most popular articulation of the quote is attributed to the Irish poet William Butler Yeats, who is supposed to have said, "Education is not filling a pail [or bucket] but lighting a fire." However, there appears to be no substantive evidence that he made this statement. It is possible that Yeats paraphrased the original insight by the Greek philosopher Plutarch, and thus was misattributed to the quote. The correct attribution belongs to Plutarch from his essay "On Listening." Plutarch wrote, "For the mind does not require filling like a bottle but rather, like wood, it only requires kindling to create in it an impulse to think independently and an ardent desire for the truth." This translation is from *Moralia* by Plutarch, volume 1 of the Loeb Classical Library edition, "De auditor" by Plutarch, 1927. Thus, I have used this version for the purposes of this book. There have been other interpretations of the general theme of the statement without attribution, one of

which is "The mind is not a vessel that needs filling, but wood that needs igniting." In whatever form it appears, the statement is still profound in emphasizing that the purpose of education and thus the role of the teacher is to inspire a love of learning and not just convey information.

CHAPTER 1

1. Norman Maclean, *A River Runs through It and Other Stories* (Chicago: University of Chicago Press, 1976), 26.

CHAPTER 2

1. The Kolb Experiential Learning Profile (KELP) is an upgrade on the Kolb Learning Style Inventory. KELP expands on the original four learning styles while emphasizing the importance of experiential learning. To gain a more in-depth perspective on KELP, review the self-assessment tool at the website of the Institute for Experiential Learning.

CHAPTER 3

1. Richard P. Feynman, *The Pleasure of Finding Things Out*, ed. Jeffrey Robbins (New York: Perseus, 1999), 14.

2. For the Post-It story, see P. Ranganath Nayak and John M. Ketteringham, *Break-Throughs! How the Vision and Drive of Innovators in Sixteen Companies Created Commercial Breakthroughs That Swept the World* (New York: Rawson Associates, 1986), 50–73.

3. For the story about Alexander Fleming's discovery of penicillin, see Susan Aldridge, John Parascandola, and Jeffrey L. Sturchio, *The Discovery and Development of Penicillin, 1928–1945* (London: Alexander Fleming Laboratory Museum, 1999), https://www.acs.org/content/dam/acsorg/education/whatischemistry/landmarks/flemingpenicillin/the-discovery-and-development-of-penicillin-commemorative-booklet.pdf.

4. For the story and video of the Tiger Woods commercial, see Cork Gaines, "The Amazing Story behind Tiger Woods' Iconic Nike Juggling Commercial," Business Insider, December 27, 2017, https://www.businessinsider.com/tiger-woods-nike-juggling-commercial-2015-12, and John Moriello, "Tiger Woods' Most Memorable Commercial Wasn't Planned," Sportscasting,

March 21, 2020, https://www.sportscasting.com/tiger-woods-most-memorable
-commercial-wasnt-planned/.

CHAPTER 4

1. Sir Ken Robinson, "Do schools kill creativity?" TED talk, YouTube video, January 7, 2007, 20:03, https://www.youtube.com/watch?v=iG9CE55wbtY.
2. Arthur Koestler, *The Act of Creation* (New York: Penguin, 1964).
3. John Keegan, "There's a better way to do it. Find it," TED talk, YouTube video, November 27, 2018, 18:53, www.youtube.com/watch?v=Vrw5brX1Wfo.
4. Movieclips, "Apollo 13 (1995)—Square Peg in a Round Hole Scene," YouTube video, 1:15, www.youtube.com/watch?v=ry55--J4_VQ.

CHAPTER 6

1. David Ahearn, Frank Ford, and David Wilk, *Happy Accidents: The Transformative Power of "Yes, And" at Work and in Life* (Hoboken, NJ: Wiley, 2017).
2. Kelly Leonard and Tom Yorton, *Yes, And: How Improvisation Reverses "No, But" Thinking and Improves Creativity and Collaboration* (New York: HarperCollins, 2015).

CHAPTER 7

1. For a discussion of the know-feel-do approach to learning strategies, see, Charles C. Bonwell, "Enhancing the Lecture: Revitalizing a Traditional Format," in Tracey E. Sutherland and Charles C. Bonwell, eds., *New Directions for Teaching and Learning*, no. 67 (San Francisco: Jossey-Bass Publishers, Fall 1996) 31–44.
2. John William Gardner, *Building Community* (Washington, DC: Independent Sector, 1991).
3. Chip Heath and Dan Heath, *Made to Stick: Why Some Ideas Survive and Others Die* (New York: Random House, 2008).
4. Jim Hayhurst Jr., *The Right Mountain: Lessons from Everest on the Real Meaning of Success* (New York: Wiley, 1996)
5. For a further discussion of the elements of credibility, see Regis McKenna, *The Regis Touch: Million-dollar Advice From America's Top Marketing Consultant* (New York: Basic Books, 1985).

CHAPTER 8

1. Peter Drucker made this comment in a meeting with the author in fall 2000.

CHAPTER 9

1. The jazz session experience was designed by Professor Minet Schindehutte at Syracuse University.

CHAPTER 10

1. For a further discussion of mentoring that refers to the Yoda factor, see Laurent A. Daloz, *Mentor: Guiding the Journey of Adult Learners* (San Francisco, CA: Jossey-Bass, 1999).

CHAPTER 11

1. Walter Isaacson, *Leonardo da Vinci* (New York: Simon & Schuster, 2017).

About the Author

In finding his calling as a teacher, **Dr. Ray Smilor** has taught at every educational level—elementary, secondary, undergraduate, graduate, doctoral, and executive. He has taught at universities in the United States and in many countries around the world. As an author, consultant, and expert in entrepreneurship, he has presented at corporate outings, spoken to national and international conferences and conventions, addressed community groups, and lectured nationally and internationally. Ray has published extensively.

Figure 1.1. Dr. Ray Smilor. *Photo by B.J. Lacasse*

He has helped to build three organizations related to teaching and training in the United States—an academic think tank at the University of Texas at Austin, the Kauffman Center for Entrepreneurial Leadership at the Kauffman Foundation, and an international economic development organization. He has served as program manager and principal investigator on major government training programs for the US Department of State in the Middle East and North Africa and for the US Agency for International Development in Russia.

Ray has been recognized as a master teacher by the international Experiential Classroom Teacher Training Program and received its Karl Vesper Pioneer Award for "distinguished achievements in advancing the discipline of entrepreneurship." He has been selected as one of the top twenty-five entrepreneurship educators in America, and he has been a featured presenter in the International Teachers' Program at the London Business School. He received the President's Award from the United States Association for Small Business and Entrepreneurship for "outstanding leadership and service." He has received awards for teaching excellence and innovation in the United States and internationally.

Ray is emeritus professor of management, entrepreneurship, and leadership at the Neeley School of Business at Texas Christian University. You can reach Ray at his website: www.raysmilor.com.